Las Vegas
2008

A Selection
*of **Restaurants** & **Hotels***

Let us know what you think.

Complete a brief survey at michelinguide.com/survey,
and we'll send you a promotion code good
for 20% off your next Michelin Maps & Guides
purchase at langenscheidt.com.

Receive updates, news, valuable discounts
and invitations to special events
by signing up at michelinguide.com/signup.

Offer expires 7/31/08.

Manufacture française des pneumatiques Michelin
Société en commandite par actions au capital de 304 000 000 EUR
Place des Carmes-Déchaux – 63000 Clermont-Ferrand (France)
R.C.S. Clermont-Fd B 855 200 507

No part of this publication may be reproduced in any form
without the prior permission of the publisher.

© **Michelin 2008, Propriétaires-éditeurs**
Dépot légal Novembre 2007

Printed in Canada
Published in 2007

Cover photograph : George Doyle/Stockbyte/Getty Images

Although the information in this guide was believed by the authors and publisher
to be accurate and current at the time of publication, they cannot accept
responsibility for any inconvenience, loss, or injury sustained by any person relying
on information or advice contained in this guide. Things change over time and
travelers should take steps to verify and confirm information, especially time-
sensitive information related to prices, hours of operation, and availability.

Please send your comments to:

Michelin North America, Inc.
Travel Publications
One Parkway South – Greenville, SC 29615 USA
Phone: 1-800-423-0485
Fax: 1-800-378-7471
www.michelintravel.com
Michelin.guides@us.michelin.com

Dear reader

I am thrilled to launch the first edition of our Michelin Guide Las Vegas. Our teams have made every effort to produce a selection that fully reflects the rich diversity of the restaurant and hotel scene in the Neon Jungle.

The Michelin Guide provides a comprehensive selection and rating, in all categories of comfort and prices. As part of our meticulous and highly confidential evaluation process, Michelin's American inspectors conducted anonymous visits to restaurants and hotels in Las Vegas. Michelin's inspectors are the eyes and ears of the customers, and thus their anonymity is key to ensure that they receive the same treatment as any other guest. The decision to award a star is a collective one, based on the consensus of all inspectors who have visited a particular establishment.

Our company's two founders, Édouard and André Michelin, published the first Michelin Guide in 1900, to provide motorists with practical information about where they could service and repair their cars, and find quality accommodations and a good meal. The star-rating system for outstanding restaurants was introduced in 1926. The same system is used for our American selections.

I sincerely hope that the Michelin Guide Las Vegas 2008 will become your favorite guide to the area's restaurants and hotels. On behalf of all our Michelin employees, let me wish you the very best enjoyment in your Vegas dining and hotel experiences.

Michel Rollier
Chief Executive Officer, Michelin

Contents

THE STRIP   24

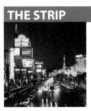

WEST OF THE STRIP 138

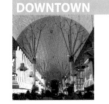

DOWNTOWN 160

🏠 Where to **stay**

To locate restaurants in selected Strip resorts, refer to floorplans in the Where To Stay section.

How to use this guide

Hotel classification according to comfort
(more pleasant if in red)

🏠 Quite comfortable
🏠🏠 Very comfortable
🏠🏠🏠🏠 Luxury in the traditional style
🏠 Comfortable
🏠🏠🏠 Top class comfort

Map References
(Hotels)

Average Prices
prices do not include applicable taxes

Price classification
(Hotels)
$ under $150
$$ $150 to $250
$$$ $250 to $350
$$$$ over $350

Hotel symbols
149
rooms No. of rooms and suites
♿ Wheelchair access
🏋 Exercise room
💆 Spa
🏊 Swimming pool
🗣 Equipped conference room

Blue Hotel

🏠🏠

320

43 Las Vegas Blvd. S. (at Flamingo Rd.)
Phone: 702-677-2664 or 866-677-2665
Fax: 702-677-2668
Web: www.bluehotel.com
Prices: $$$$

149 Rooms
23 Suites
♿
🏋
💆🏊

The Strip ▶ Blue Hotel

Palazzo

🏠🏠🏠

065

43 Las Vegas Blvd. S. (at Spring Mountain Rd.)
Phone: 702-677-2664 or 866-677-2665
Fax: 702-677-2668
Web: Web: www.palazzo.com
Prices: $$$

149 Rooms
23 Suites
♿
🏋
💆
🏊
🗣

Although you may not be planning to get a whole lot of sleep while visiting Las Vegas, the Palazzo is the ideal place to relax. This hotel is located right in the center of all of the Las Vegas Strip action. With 8 pools, 400 guest rooms and 10 spas, you will definitely find what you are looking for.

Rooms provide complimentary bath amenities, plush robes, large flat-screen TVs and wireless internet connection. When you do take a break from the glimmer and lights of The Strip, you can find peace and quiet in your comfy king-size bed. Sore muscles can be revived in the two-person hot tub, a standard amenity in each of the hotels guest rooms.

Tired of eating out? Order room service from one of Palazzo's 9 restaurants, offering cuisine types from Burmese to Vietnamese.

Don't miss the world's largest roller coaster, which runs throughout the lobby of the hotel.

Where to eat...

▶ RECOMMENDED

ams ⊙⊙⊙	⅄⅄⅄	132
Chesney	⅄⅄	133
Ellsworth	⅄⅄	135
JL's Pantry	⅄⅄	140
Lynn-Dee	⅄	143
Simpsons	⅄	152

▶ ALSO
Ernie's Bistro
Ila
Jonny-Moe

The Strip

214

215

Las Vegas areas
Each area is color coded...

■ The Strip ■ West of The Strip
■ East of The Strip ■ Downtown

Restaurants within a Strip megaresort.

Strip megaresort

6

Restaurants classification according to comfort (more pleasant if in red)	✗ Quite comfortable ✗✗ Comfortable	✗✗✗ Very comfortable ✗✗✗✗ Top class comfort	✗✗✗✗✗ Luxury in the traditional style

Name, address and information about the establishment

Map References (Restaurants)

Price classification (Restaurants)
- ⊚ under $25
- $$ $25 to $50
- $$$ $50 to $75
- $$$$ over $75

Las Vegas area

Hotel within which the restaurant resides

Ellsworth (Palazzo)

Italian ✗✗

002

888 Las Vegas Blvd. S. (at Tropicana Ave.)

Phone:	702-553-0004 or 866-553-0005	Tue - Fri lunch & dinner
Fax:	702-553-0006	Sat - Sun dinner only
e-mail:	ellsworth@hotmail.com	
Web:	www.ellsworth-eatery.com	
Prices:	$$$	

The Strip ▶ Palazzo

The Strip

ams (Palazzo) ✿✿✿

Seafood ✗✗✗✗

003

222 E. Sahara Ave. (at Tropicana Ave.)

Phone:	702-677-0001 or 865-677-0002	Lunch & dinner daily
Fax:	702-677-0003	
Web:	www.ams-restaurant.com	
Prices:	$$$	

Step into the Italian Restaurant and feel like you have taken a trip to Italy without ever leaving the city. It's no wonder that this restaurant, with its main dining room lighted with 750 custom candles, and set with Limoges china and Baroque-style furnishings, is prized for an enchanting evening out.

In this sanctuary of classic Italian cuisine, you can choose your own dishes within the framework of a three-, four-, or five-course prix-fixe menu. Although it constantly changes, the selection includes a long list of Italian favorites (Spaghetti Bolognese, White Pizza and Gnocchi), many interpreted with local products. For non-meat eaters, a vegetarian tasting menu is always an option.

On the wine list, you'll discover an excellent selection of Italian varietals, including Chianti from the chef's native Puglia region.

Appetizers	Entrées	Desserts
• Seafood Salad	• Hamburger with Blue Cheese	• Crème Brûlée
• Spicy Shrimp	• Macaroni and Cheese	• Tiramisu
• Seared Tuna	• Grilled Chicken in a Peach Sauce	• Coconut Cake

n spot for more than
ow operates under the
Bill Smith. It's no wonder
s romantic main dining
ustom candles, and set
uis XVI-style furnishings,
evening out.
French cuisine, you can
ithin the framework of a
prix-fixe menu. Although
election includes a long
pered filet mignon with
uail stuffed with ris de
), many interpreted with
eat eaters, a vegetarian
ption.
discover an excellent
tals, including Riesling
ace region, as well as
ordeaux.

135

Star for good food
✿ to ✿✿✿

Restaurant symbols
- 🍽 Cash only
- ♿ Wheelchair access
- 🌳 Garden or terrace dining
- 🍷 A particularly interesting wine list
- 👔 Jacket required
- 🚗 Valet parking
- 🌙 Late dining

Sample menu for starred restaurants

How to use this guide

A Brief History of Las Vegas

America's fastest growing metro area, Las Vegas claimed just shy of 39 million visitors in 2006. Whether they come here to shop, be entertained or just to gamble, many are betting on discovering good food as well as fortune.

THE MEADOWS

Some 12 thousand years ago, a lush marsh thrived in what is now the Nevada desert. In 1829, a Mexican scouting party stumbled on an oasis fed by ancient springs, calling it Las Vegas, "the meadows." Though the Mormons were the first group to actually settle in the area (in 1855), it was the advent of the railroad that led to the founding of Las Vegas on May 15, 1905.

Construction of the railroad and Hoover Dam turned Vegas into another kind of watering hole. In the 1930s, legalized gambling (with no regulations) created fertile ground for organized crime and fostered the town's no-holds-barred reputation. Casinos sprang up downtown to accommodate the serious gamblers who were flooding into the area. In 1941 El Rancho resort opened on a lonely length of highway leading to downtown, triggering a spate of building on the stretch now known as "The Strip." Glamour came too, in the form of the Flamingo Hotel, a ritzy "carpet joint" founded by mobster Benjamin "Bugsy" Siegel in 1946. Hard on the Flamingo's heels followed the Tropicana, the Stardust, and the Sands, where the famed Rat Pack performed. Sin City was in full swing.

Feeding the early iniquity were prodigious quantities of chuck-wagon chow. In an effort to keep guests on the property throughout the

©Mark Gibson

©Mark Gibson

night, El Rancho's owner laid out a "Midnight Chuck Wagon Buffet" (all you could eat for a dollar), birthing a popular dining concept that continues—albeit with posh theme décor and freshly made offerings—to this day.

CORPORATE CAPITAL AND CELEBRITY CHEFS

In the late 1960s, legal reform allowed publicly traded corporations to obtain gambling licenses, adding to the Vegas boom. But 20 years later, casino-style gambling arrived in Atlantic City, New Jersey, and suddenly Las Vegas had some competition. Indeed, everything seemed as if it had been on the buffet a little too long. Enter entrepreneur Steve Wynn, who changed the face of Vegas when he built the city's first mega-resort, the 3,044-room,

$630-million Mirage, in 1989. Soon the old hotels were being imploded right and left, making way for fantastic new properties where one could joust with King Arthur, walk like an Egyptian, dine in the Eiffel Tower, or take a gondola ride along Venice's Grand Canal.

Toque trumped toga when Wolfgang Puck came to Caesars Palace in 1992, and celebrity chefs have been hedging their bets in Vegas ever since. Especially with the recent arrival of two of France's most esteemed chefs, Guy Savoy and Joël Robuchon, the city is being heralded as a culinary destination—and a pricey one at that.

So while Sin City's past— culinary and otherwise— may be a little unsavory, Las Vegas is raising the stakes for a full-flavored future. That you'll find plenty of great restaurants in town is already a sure bet.

Where to **eat**

Alphabetical list of Restaurants

Where to **eat** ▶ Alphabetical list of Restaurants

Restaurants by Cuisine Type

Where to eat ▶ Restaurants by Cuisine Type

13

Hawaiian

Indian

International

Italian

Japanese

Mediterranean

Mexican

Moroccan

Seafood

Southwestern

Spanish

Steakhouse

Thai

Cuisine Type by area

Where to **eat** ▶ Cuisine Type by area

15

Where to **eat** ▶ Cuisine Type by area

Live in Italian

At finer restaurants in Los Angeles, Melbourne, Cape Town and of course, Positano.

Starred Restaurants

*W*ithin the selection we offer you, some restaurants deserve to be highlighted for their particularly good cuisine. When giving one, two or three Michelin stars, there are a number of things that we judge, including the quality of the ingredients, the technical skill and flair that goes into their preparation, the blend and clarity of flavors, and the balance of the menu. Just as important is the ability to produce excellent cooking time and again. We make as many visits as we need, so that our readers can be sure of quality and consistency.

A two- or three-star restaurant has to offer something very special in its cuisine; a real element of creativity, originality or "personality" that sets it apart from the rest. Three stars —our highest award—are given to the very best restaurants, where the whole dining experience is superb.

Cuisine in any style, modern or traditional, may be eligible for a star. Because we apply the same independent standards everywhere, the awards have become benchmarks of reliability and excellence in more than 20 European countries, particularly in France, where we have awarded stars for almost 80 years, and where the expression "Now that's real three-star quality!" has entered into the language.

The awarding of a star is based solely on the quality of the cuisine.

✿✿✿

Exceptional cuisine, worth a special journey.

One always eats here extremely well, sometimes superbly.
Distinctive dishes are precisely executed, using superlative
ingredients.

Joël Robuchon	XXXX	61

✿✿

Excellent cuisine, worth a detour.

Skillfully and carefully crafted dishes of outstanding quality.

Alex	XXXXX	26
Guy Savoy	XXXX	57
Picasso	XXXX	79

✿

A very good restaurant in its category.

A place offering cuisine prepared to a consistently high
standard.

Alizé	XXX	140
Andre's (Downtown)	XX	162
Aureole	XXX	29
Bradley Ogden	XXX	35
Daniel Boulud Brasserie	XXX	44
L'Atelier de Joël Robuchon	XX	63
Le Cirque	XXX	64
Mesa Grill	XX	65
Michael Mina	XXX	66
miX	XXX	67
Nobu	XX	128
Wing Lei	XXXX	106

Where to **eat** ▶ **Starred Restaurants**

Buffets

In the days before Las Vegas became an oasis of fine dining, buffets were the favored dining choice at Las Vegas hotels, catering to crowds who subscribe to the philosophy that more is more insofar as food is concerned. If you're staying at a resort on or near The Strip, chances are your hotel offers a buffet. These all-you-can-eat abbondanzas typically feature enormous dining rooms and a wide array of cuisines arranged at different stations, where patrons serve themselves to as many helpings as their appetite will allow. Advertising a reasonable price tag, these groaning boards are normally open for breakfast, lunch and dinner. Lunch usually runs under $20 per person, and dinner rolls in at less than $30. Beverage service is included, with the exception of alcoholic beverages.

In recent years, buffets have traded rows of chafing dishes, heat lamps and steam tables for impressive food displays, diverse ethnic options, and even dishes cooked to order in some cases. Items span the globe and run the gamut from fried chicken and prime rib to sushi, tacos and crêpes. For those who find it difficult to tear themselves away from the casino to eat, the game of Keno is frequently available in many buffet dining rooms.

The following is a brief list of buffets that meets our standards of good quality and value.

The Strip

West of The Strip

Where to **eat** ▶ Buffets

Where to eat for less than $25

Where to have a late dinner

Restaurants taking last orders after 10:30pm at least four nights a week.

A.J.'s Steakhouse	112	Mon Ami Gabi	68
Aquaknox	28	N9NE	151
B & B Ristorante	30	Nobu	128
Bradley Ogden	35	Noodles	70
Café Ba Ba Reeba	36	Noodle Shop (The)	71
China Grill	39	Nove Italiano	153
808	48	Origin India	130
Empress Court	50	P.F. Chang's	76
Ferraro's	145	Pink Taco	133
Fin	52	Rao's	83
Firefly	115	Red 8	84
Gaylord India	147	rm seafood	85
Grand Lux Cafe	55	Smith & Wollensky	91
Hofbräuhaus	118	Social House	92
Hyakumi	58	STACK	94
Isla	60	Tao	99
J.C. Wooloughan	149	Taqueria Cañonita	100
Lindo Michoacán	120	Trevi	103
Mesa Grill	65	Valentino	104
miX	67		

The Strip

To locate restaurants in selected Strip resorts, refer to floorplans in the Where To Stay section.

THE STRIP

A carnival of neon lights and eye-popping architecture, The Strip boasts the city's largest collection of resorts and casinos. All this lies along a 4.5-mile stretch of Las Vegas Boulevard that begins at Stratosphere and runs south to Mandalay Bay (the 2000 to 4000 blocks).

THE DESERT BLOSSOMS

When the first casinos sprang up Downtown, the boulevard now known as The Strip was a vacant length of Highway 91 south of the business district. The first hotel to go up here after the Nevada legislature legalized gambling in 1931 was El Rancho Vegas. By choosing this location, owner Thomas Hull could avoid taxes and restrictions on buildings within city limits. His 1941 hotel was closely followed by The Last Frontier and the Flamingo Hotel, mobster Bugsy Siegel's famous "carpet joint." By the early 1950s, the Las Vegas Strip—so named by police officer and owner of The Last Frontier, Guy McAfee—began to come into its own as venues like the now-defunct Sands, The Dunes and The Stardust raised their heads.

AN ERA OF EXTRAVAGANCE

Resorts along The Strip started eclipsing the Downtown venues in the '60s, but it wasn't until

©Mark Gibson

24

1989 that the first megaresort opened on Las Vegas Boulevard. Steve Wynn's Mirage, complete with a lava-spewing volcano out front and tropical gardens and waterfalls inside, introduced a new era of extravagant casino resorts.

The past two decades have seen The Strip soar with amazing hotels, whose profiles range from a 30-story pyramid and a scale model of the Eiffel Tower to Steve Wynn's eponymous, 50-story curvilinear glass tower. A monorail now connects properties along the east side of Las Vegas Boulevard, running from The Sahara to MGM Grand.

Entertainment, too, has changed over the years, from Rat Pack crooners Frank Sinatra, Dean Martin and Sammy Davis Jr. to headliners Celine Dion, Elton John and a host of young pop singers.

Today The Strip's megaresorts are cities unto themselves, self-sustaining with luxurious guestrooms, plush casinos, fine restaurants, spas, shopping arcades, theaters, lush pool environments and just about anything else your heart desires. The Vegas skyline is rising ever higher with projects like the new City Center, currently under construction on The Strip between Bellagio and the Monte Carlo. Scheduled for completion by the end of 2009, this sleek multi-use urban complex will comprise condominiums, casino hotels, and plenty of space for retail, dining and entertainment.

Alex ✿✿ (Wynn)

001

Contemporary XXXXX

3131 Las Vegas Blvd. S.

Phone: 702-770-3300
Web: www.wynnlasvegas.com
Prices: $$$$

Tue – Sat dinner only

Wynn Las Vegas

Alex is the kind of place you want to go to impress a date, pop an important question or wine and dine VIP clients. Who wouldn't be impressed descending the marble staircase into this comely room clad in soft flounces of copper-colored draperies and lit by shimmering crystal chandeliers?

Credit Alessandro Stratta's Italian-French heritage for inspiring the chef's refined cooking. "Riviera cuisine," as the restaurant bills it, boils down to contemporary French food with a soupçon of Italian influence stirred in for good measure. Whether you go with the tasting menu or order à la carte, the chef and his staff blend clear focus and expert technique into every dish, lightly breading frogs' legs and dousing them with a sublime white-wine butter sauce; or scattering heirloom peas, carrots and morels around a fillet of John Dory to sing the praises of spring.

Appetizers

- Marinated Kampachi, Osetra Caviar, Coconut-Cucumber Custard
- Sea Scallops, White Asparagus, Pink Grapefruit, Sea Urchin
- Veal Sweetbreads, Fettuccine "Carbonara", Parmigiano

Entrées

- Daurade "Royale", Rhubarb, Sweet and Sour Orange
- Atlantic Bass, Fennel, Tomatoes, Olives, Basil-Lemon Sauce
- Spring Lamb, Purple Artichokes, Pancetta, Spring Garlic

Desserts

- Strawberries and Mascarpone Cream and Brown Butter Cake
- White and Dark Chocolate Napoleon and Milk Chocolate Ice Cream

Andre's (Monte Carlo)

French ✗✗✗

002

3770 Las Vegas Blvd. S.

Phone: 702-798-7151
Web: www.andrelv.com
Prices: $$$$

Dinner daily

Comstock/Jupiter Images

The Strip

Middle and most elegant sibling in André Rochat's family of three Las Vegas restaurants, Andre's at the Monte Carlo succeeds in its aim to re-create the ambience of a Renaissance-era French château. From the recessed, hand-painted ceiling and the Versace chargers to the crimson U-shaped booths that nuzzle intimate alcoves along the perimeter of the small room, the décor bespeaks a tranquility centuries removed from the modern world.

Classic, uncomplicated, and French at their core, the recipes here lean more toward the contemporary (think pan-roasted diver scallops with celery-root purée) than the menu at the original Andre's Downtown. Courses wheeled to the table on carts, and plates covered by silver domes represent formal but not stuffy service, which pays special attention to detail.

A circular staircase winds upstairs to the two-story, glassed-in wine cellar.

Aquaknox (Venetian)

003

Seafood ✗✗✗

3355 Las Vegas Blvd. S.

Phone:	702-414-3772
Web:	www.aquaknox.net
Prices:	**$$$**

Dinner daily

E Brands Restaurants

Shimmering like the sea in cool deep blues and silver accents, Aquaknox shines the spotlight on "global water cuisine." Chef Tom Moloney, a protégé of Wolfgang Puck, trolls the world's oceans for the freshest catch and flies the likes of Louisiana prawns, John Dory, New Zealand King salmon, and day-boat scallops to his desert oasis.

The large lounge area in the entry presents a dazzling raw bar where you can impress any guest—or date—with the seafood plateau for two: a shellfish abbondanza piled high with mussels, oyster, prawns, clams, ceviche, lobster, stone-crab claws, and ponzu oyster sliders. Wines are plucked from the cylindrical, walk-in cellar, which is surrounded by a rushing water wall at the front of the restaurant.

If you want a glimpse of the action, request a table in the back dining area, near the exhibition kitchen.

Aureole ✿ (Mandalay Bay)

Contemporary ✗✗✗

3950 Las Vegas Blvd. S.

Dinner daily

Phone: 702-632-7401
Web: www.aureolelv.com
Prices: $$$$

The Charlie Palmer Group

Dinner and a show is the classic Vegas entertainment, and at Charlie Palmer's Aureole you'll enjoy both. The show here centers on the striking stainless-steel and glass wine tower, which rises toward the ceiling in the dining area. Some 10,000 bottles cool their heels inside this temperature- and humidity-controlled facility.

How does someone manage to retrieve wine four stories up? The answer is Charlie's angels. Inspired by a scene in the film *Mission Impossible*, aerobatic wine stewards navigate inside the tower by means of mechanical hoists. Each "wine angel" is equipped with an intercom and a holster to hold wine bottles.

Palmer's nightly offerings interpret contemporary cuisine with studied French flair. The more elaborate of the two nightly multicourse menus will set you back a buck or two hundred (if you add wine pairings), but it's worth the price for such a heavenly experience.

Appetizers

- Pinot Noir-poached Seckel Pear Charlotte with Foie Gras Torchon
- Alaskan King Crab Legs over Green and White Asparagus
- Hawaiian Hamachi Duo

Entrées

- Seared Ahi Tuna, Citron Potato Gratin, Sauté of Spring Peas
- Roast Loin of Veal, Chanterelles, Rustic Yukon Golds
- Roast Rack of Colorado Lamb, Stuffed Campari Tomato

Desserts

- Tasting of Pistachio and Meyer Lemon
- Strawberry Rhubarb Frangipane Tart with Vanilla Bean Panna Cotta
- Dark Chocolate Mint Bar with Peppermint Ice Cream Terrine

B & B Ristorante (Venetian)

Italian ✗✗

3355 Las Vegas Blvd. S.

Phone:	702-266-9977	Dinner daily
Web:	www.bandbristorante.com	
Prices:	$$$	

Joe Vaughn

It was only a matter of time until chef Mario Batali added his culinary can-can—performed, of course, in his signature orange Crocs—to the Sin City restaurant lineup. His first Vegas venture, with its dark woods and wall of wine cabinets, has been kicking up a fuss at the Venetian since it opened in spring 2007.

Rustic finesse marks the regional Italian specialties. Tender, smoky grilled octopus paired with marinated borlotti beans and limoncello vinaigrette makes an excellent introduction to *secondi* such as mint "love letters" filled with lamb sausage, and grilled lamb chops *"Scottadita,"* served with eggplant and lemon yogurt. Service is as highly polished as the silverware, and the wine list high-steps with Italian varietals—especially Barolo and Barbaresco.

As an encore, Batali followed with casual Enoteca San Marco, located upstairs in the Grand Canal Shoppes.

Bartolotta (Wynn)

Italian

3131 Las Vegas Blvd. S.

		Dinner daily
Phone:	702-770-9966	
Web:	www.wynnlasvegas.com	
Prices:	$$$$	

The Strip

Wynn Las Vegas

Fishing for fine seafood in Las Vegas? You need cast your line no farther than the Esplanade at Wynn, where Bartolotta will fill the bill swimmingly. Follow the winding staircase down into the main dining room, an ocean of opulence awash in smooth marble and rich fabrics.

Paul Bartolotta, former chef and managing partner at Chicago's popular Spiagga, brings his love of Italian cuisine to his kitchen in the desert. Here his heritage and affinity for wild-caught seafood results in a menu that flaunts whole fish flown in fresh daily from the waters surrounding Italy. Although it's pricey to order a whole fish ($14 for 3 ounces), you'll nonetheless net the likes of perfectly baked, delicate Mediterranean snapper, served tableside with a flourish.

For the *ne plus ultra* in romance, request one of the tented cabana tables that circle the tranquil pool outside.

BOA Steakhouse (Caesars Palace)

Steakhouse ✗✗

The Forum Shops, 3500 Las Vegas Blvd. S.

Phone: 702-733-7373
Web: www.innovativedining.com
Prices: $$$

Lunch & dinner daily

©Jeff Green/Innovative Dining

BOA is not your grandfather's steakhouse. Forget about the dark wood paneling and clubby atmosphere; this place exudes a younger and hipper vibe, worthy of its setting on the top floor of the Forum Shops. Think ghostly trees of sandblasted driftwood that "grow" out of the center of the room, padded ultrasuede walls, and a towering glass-enclosed wine cellar, and you've got the feel of BOA.

If you're a steakhouse fan, the menu will look familiar. New York strip steak dry-aged for 40 days vies with premium Japanese Wagyu beef and Kobe flatiron steak for your attention. Here, the signature surf and turf features a lobster tail and the Kobe steak of the day served with Hudson Valley foie gras. All entrées come with your choice or rubs or crusts, and sauces.

Had a bad day at the tables? The three-course fixed-price market menu may be your best bet, price-wise, for dinner.

Border Grill (Mandalay Bay)

008

3950 Las Vegas Blvd. S.

Phone: 702-632-7403

Web: www.bordergrill.com

Prices: **$$**

Lunch & dinner daily

The Strip

MGM Mirage

You'll find the Vegas outpost of Mary Sue Milliken and Susan Feniger's Santa Monica flagship located on the walkway between Mandalay Bay's convention center and the main casino floor. While the Sin City sibling may lack a bit of the stylistic boldness of the California original, Border Grill Las Vegas maintains the upbeat Latin music, the casual atmosphere, and the well-prepared Mexican cuisine that mark its older sister.

This is one of the few restaurants in Mandalay Bay that's open for lunch, making classics like plantain empanadas and green corn tamales a sure bet with the convention crowd. In the evening, groups of friends looking for a party seek out Border Grill for its tasty *bocaditos* (small bites) and margaritas menu.

Patios on both levels of the restaurant face the pools of Mandalay Bay, where hotel guests can take advantage of poolside take-out service.

Bouchon (Venetian)

009

3355 Las Vegas Blvd. S.

Phone:	702-414-6200	Mon – Fri dinner only
Web:	www.venetian.com	Sat – Sun lunch & dinner
Prices:	$$	

© Deborah Jones

Cousin of Thomas Keller's original Bouchon in the Napa Valley, the Venetian's rendition is similar in many respects. Both restaurants share the same menu, with one exception: the Vegas Bouchon is open for breakfast. This isn't your standard hotel breakfast, though; the menu here features quiche, *boudin blanc, croque madame* and baked eggs Florentine—not to mention fresh-baked brioches and flaky chocolate croissants. Dinner adds standard bistro *plats principaux* from steak *frites* and *poulet rôti* (roasted chicken) to trout amandine and gnocchi *à la Parisienne*.

With its pewter bar, mosaic-tile floor, and hand-painted murals, Bouchon's setting in the Venezia Tower will make you long for lingering meals in Lyon—minus the palm trees, of course, which are unique to this desert locale.

If you're hoping to have lunch here, you'll have to come on a weekend.

Bradley Ogden ✿ (Caesars Palace)

010

3570 Las Vegas Blvd. S.

Phone: 702-731-7731   Dinner daily

Web: www.caesarspalace.com

Prices: $$$$

The Strip

© Gary Moss / Caesars Palace

In spring 2003, chef Bradley Ogden gambled on his first establishment outside California when he opened this 8,000-square-foot restaurant in Caesars Palace. Lady Luck seems to have smiled on him, since the place is still going strong.

The chef owes his success to more than just luck. Modern and airy, sober and sleek, Bradley Ogden's space begins with a bar and lounge and opens into two adjacent dining rooms. Here, Ogden's son Bryan chooses top-quality ingredients from farms around the country and combines them in winning ways. A classic touch tempers the kitchen's modern approach to ultra-fresh products such as North Carolina shrimp, Wisconsin pheasant, and Eden Farms pork loin.

In a hurry to get back to the game? Grab a seat at the bar, where you can have a quick ground-steak burger, Barron Point oysters on the half shell, or—of course—a Caesar salad.

Appetizers	*Entrées*	*Desserts*
● Bigeye Sashimi, Caramelized Hearts of Palm, Marinated Watermelon	● Atlantic Halibut, Monterey Squid, Chickpeas	● Vanilla Angel Food Cake, Macerated Raspberries
● Yellow Corn Soup, Maine Lobster, Paula's Lemon Verbena	● Oak Grilled South Dakota Bison, Brown Bread Gnocchi, Morels	● White Chocolate Cheesecake, Bing Cherries
	● Ribeye, Maytag Blue Cheese Soufflé, Heirloom Beets	● Mango Sorbet, Elderflower Soup, Blue Basil Buds

Café Ba Ba Reeba

011

Spanish ✗

Fashion Show Mall, 3200 Las Vegas Blvd. S.
(at Spring Mountain Rd.)

Phone: 702-258-1211   Lunch & dinner daily
Web: www.cafebabareeba.com
Prices: ⊜⊜

Cafe Ba-Ba-Reeba!

This tapas bar branched out from its original location
in Chicago's Lincoln Park to add Latin panache to the
ground floor of Fashion Show Mall on the Vegas Strip.
A party spirit prevails at the fun and casual place,
enlivened by loud Latin music and a large bar, where
sherry flights, martinis and a half a dozen different
sangrias complement the list of Spanish wines.

Sharing is the way to go at Ba Ba Reeba. Start with
an assortment of hot and cold tapas for the table,
and move on to a hearty paella, a selection of *toro
brochetas* (vertical skewers of meat or seafood), or
perhaps a *caldero*, a stew (made with rice, savory
broth and meat or seafood) named for the traditional
cast-iron kettle in which it is served.

When you're tired of the megahotels, Cafe Ba Ba Reeba
provides a good alternative, with reasonable prices to
boot.

The Capital Grille

012

Fashion Show Mall, 3200 Las Vegas Blvd. S.
(at Spring Mountain Rd.)

Phone:	702-932-6631	Mon – Sat lunch & dinner
Web:	www.thecapitalgrille.com	Sun dinner only
Prices:	$$$	

The Strip

The Capital Grille

Part of a chain with locations across the country, including Denver, Detroit, New York City and Washington, DC, The Capital Grille has added Vegas as a notch in its culinary belt. You'll find the Sin City satellite on the third level of Fashion Show Mall, just across the street from Wynn Las Vegas.

There, in an Art Deco ambience enhanced by mahogany, copper and low lighting, you'll enjoy classic steakhouse fare, spotlighting dry-aged beef. Sliced filet mignon with cippollini onions and sautéed wild mushrooms wins raves, while the Grille's Delmonico—a 22-ounce bone-in ribeye—or the hefty broiled lobster (sized from two to five pounds) will appeal to big winners with equally big appetites. Sides range from the requisite creamed spinach to cottage fries topped with satisfyingly crispy Vidalia onion strings.

Charlie Palmer Steak (Four Seasons)

013

Steakhouse ✗✗✗

3960 Las Vegas Blvd. S.

Phone: 702-632-5120
Web: www.charliepalmer.com
Prices: $$$$

Dinner daily

&

The Charlie Palmer Group

You won't have to traipse through a clanging casino to access this clubby restaurant, housed off the lobby of the elegant Four Seasons hotel, at the south end of the Strip. Charlie Palmer's second restaurant in Las Vegas (the first was Aureole at Mandalay Bay next door) uses leafy plants, varnished woods and gold tones to add warmth to the spacious dining room.

All beef here, from the grilled filet mignon to the hefty 22-ounce Kansas City ribeye, is dry-aged certified Black Angus. Stuffed Maine lobster and a smattering of fish entrées will satisfy those with a hankering for seafood. Expect sauces and sides, like the truffled baked potato, to cost you extra.

Looking for more lively digs? Sink into one of the comfy sofas in the boisterous cigar-friendly lounge, where you can nurse a cocktail and listen to live music on Friday and Saturday nights.

China Grill (Mandalay Bay)

014

3950 Las Vegas Blvd. S.

Phone: 702-632-7404
Web: www.chinagrillmgt.com
Prices: $$$$

Dinner daily

The Strip

China Grill

A neo-Asian concept that's a surefire recipe for success, China Grill is part of a group of restaurants (under the auspices of Jeffrey Chodorow's China Grill Management) that started in Manhattan and now extends as far away as Mexico City.

Expressing a wide array of influences from across Asia, the menu is designed for sharing. Lively groups of conventioneers and clusters of friends alike find China Grill classics such as pan-seared spicy tuna (served with a *wakame* seaweed salad flavored with fragrant sesame oil), lobster pancakes, and sweet soy-marinated skirt steak perfect for sampling around the table.

Guests enter the restaurant across a glass bridge that spans a trickling water feature. Inside, a sexy, dimly lit lounge caters to the cocktail crowd, while the multilevel dining room sports a futuristic look with its planetarium-style illuminated ceiling.

Chinois (Caesars Palace)

Asian ✕

015

The Forum Shops, 3500 Las Vegas Blvd. S.

Phone:	702-737-9700	Lunch & dinner daily
Web:	www.wolfgangpuck.com	
Prices:	$$	

The Wolfgang Puck Fine Dining Group

East meets the Old West at Chinois. Located in the Forum Shops, Chinois is the little sister of the original Chinois on Main, which opened in Santa Monica in 1998. Like its sibling, the Vegas outpost honors the original concept with its modernized Hong Kong and Cantonese cuisine. The menu gallops from sushi to banana spring rolls, and from Szechuan noodles to Wolfgang Puck signatures (steamed filet of Hong Kong salmon served with a citrus-soy sauce atop stir-fried vegetables, or the ever-popular Chinois chicken salad dressed in a sweet mustard-ginger vinaigrette). Dishes are done family-style, so corral a hungry crowd and chow down to your heart's content. Tea lovers will appreciate the excellent selection of premium blends.

Sleek and spacious, the bi-level main room incorporates Asian artifacts in its design, as well as an indoor terrace for people-watching.

Corsa Cucina (Wynn)

016

3131 Las Vegas Blvd. S.

Phone:	702-770-2040	Dinner daily
Web:	www.wynnlasvegas.com	
Prices:	$$	

The Strip

Wynn Las Vegas

White leather demilune benches sidle up to oval tables in the front room of casual-chic Corsa Cucina, set on the perimeter of Wynn's casino floor. At lunch, only this front half of the restaurant and its bar are open; it's not until dinnertime that you can sit in the more secluded back room that runs the length of the semi-open kitchen.

No matter. Either way you'll enjoy a strong menu of Italian fare (think panini or grilled pizzette for lunch; duck meatballs in natural gravy with hand-cut egg fettucini or Provini veal Parmigiano for dinner) sparked by bold flavors and traditional ingredients.

A word to the wise: save room for dessert here. *Dolci,* such as the dense, semisweet chocolate tartufo, garnished with buttery tuiles encasing slices of caramelized banana, are as enticing to the eyes as they are to the taste buds.

The Country Club (Wynn)

American ✕✕

3131 Las Vegas Blvd. S.

Phone: 702-770-3315   Lunch & dinner daily
Web: www.wynnlasvegas.com
Prices: $$$$

The Strip

Wynn Las Vegas

The Country Club makes an equally good stop whether you're refueling before trying your luck on the back nine, or simply taking a break from power shopping in the Wynn Esplanade. Golfer or not, it's hard to resist Steve Wynn's interpretation of an upscale golf club, which manages to feel airy, despite the dark woods, plaid carpet and granite-topped tables. Maybe that's because the restaurant enjoys panoramas of the resort's lush rolling fairways and 18th-hole waterfall through a wall of tall windows.

"American steakhouse" is what the club calls itself, although its menu drives way beyond traditional steakhouse fare. Roasted-corn chowder, poured tableside, is a great way to tee off, before diving into a hefty New York strip steak or a moist fillet of grilled fish.

On warm, sunny days, tables on the outdoor patio are par for the course.

Craftsteak (MGM Grand)

Steakhouse XXX

3799 Las Vegas Blvd. S.

Phone:	702-891-7318	Dinner daily
Web:	www.mgmgrand.com	
Prices:	$$$$	

MGM Mirage

The Strip

Celebrity chef Tom Colicchio plies his craft at MGM Grand's Studio Walk shopping promenade. A mix-and-match steakhouse concept, which spawned a second location in New York City, the Vegas Craftsteak has a masculine, organic feel fed by earth tones, leather and polished wood.

Food-wise, the principle is simple: straightforward dishes are cast from premium-quality products such as grass-fed beef and heirloom vegetables, without unnecessary garnishes or sauces. The menu is organized first into categories of ingredients (meat, vegetables, fish and shellfish), then into method of preparation (roasted, fried, braised, grilled). This way you can fashion your meal, as the Bard would say, as you like it. If that's too much work, the chef's market and Kobe beef tastings dispel any guesswork.

The expansive list of wine labels ranges in price from affordable to over the top.

Daniel Boulud Brasserie ✿
(Wynn)

019

French 🍴🍴🍴

3131 Las Vegas Blvd. S.

Phone: 702-248-3463   Dinner daily
Web: www.wynnlasvegas.com
Prices: $$$

Wynn Las Vegas

With its sensuous curves and lovely lakeside location, Daniel Boulud's tony brasserie does Wynn Las Vegas proud. Nature figures prominently in the airy design, encompassing features like the metal leaf sculpture on the ceiling of the Oval Room, and the floral-themed tapestry that decorates the Salon. Light filters in through the large windows overlooking Wynn's hypnotic Lake of Dreams, where a 140-foot mountain of cascading water dazzles diners with a multimedia special-effects show twice an hour.

Equally dazzling, the straightforward brasserie fare pleases Francophile palates with dishes from *moules frites* (served only Tuesday through Saturday to ensure the freshness of the mussels) to *pissaladière*. Of course, the chef's signature NY DB burger (decadently stuffed with braised short ribs, foie gras and black truffle) is a menu mainstay. Don't pass up the elegant desserts.

Appetizers	*Entrées*	*Desserts*
• Tomato Tarte Tatin, Goat Cheese, Arugula, Basil Pesto	• Olive Oil-poached Halibut, Fleur de Courgette Farcie	• Raspberry Pistachio Tart, Sablé Breton, Lavender Honey Chantilly
• "Maryland Crab Bake", Heirloom Tomatoes, Spicy Lemon Aïoli	• Short Ribs en Daube Provençale, Carrot Mousseline	• Guanaja Chocolate Charlotte, Coffee Liqueur Lady Fingers
	• Bacon-crusted, Kurobuta Pork Chop	

David Burke (Venetian)

020

3355 Las Vegas Blvd. S.

Phone: 702-414-7111   Dinner daily
Web: www.davidburkelasvegas.net
Prices: $$$

E Brands Restaurants

Next door to Aquaknox and near the Venetian's conference rooms, David Burke is a newcomer to the Vegas epicurean arena. The restaurant is named for its founder, the New York City chef whose bold takes on American cuisine culminate in signatures such as the "crisp and angry lobster cocktail" appetizer (a pound of lobster, deep fried, cut into large chunks and doused with hot oil infused with toasted chile powder) and Peking duck David Burke (a bed of stir-fried vegetables and chow fun noodles topped with slices of roasted Peking duck and a sunny-side-up duck egg). Typical of a town in which excess rules, hearty portions and ultra-rich desserts here are not for the faint of appetite.

Done in reds, dark woods, and white leather chairs, the casual-chic dining room centers on a free-falling "waterfall" that rains down on a sculpture constructed of red glass.

Diego (MGM Grand)

021

3799 Las Vegas Blvd. S.

Dinner daily

Phone: 702-891-3200
Web: www.mgmgrand.com
Prices: $$$

The Strip

MGM Mirage

Round up some friends and make your way to this lively Mexican restaurant at the far end of Studio Walk. Casual and boisterous, done in hot colors (bright pink, tangerine, neon green) that are as loud as the salsa music, Diego promises tons of fun, south-of-the-border style. The bar is a popular place to meet and greet; bet on the extensive list of tequilas to wash away any gaming woes.

Start with the house guacamole, prepared tableside, or the shrimp cocktail—citrus-poached rock shrimp, mixed in a cocktail shaker at your table with freshly squeezed lime juice and prickly-pear ice, before being poured into a martini glass layered with diced avocado, fresh salsa, fried corn kernels and toasted pumpkin seeds. Then move on to copious portions of signature dishes like *carne asada à la Oaxaca* (ribeye steak bathed in flavorful mole), or fiery shrimp Diablo.

Eiffel Tower (Paris)

French XXX

3655 Las Vegas Blvd. S.

Phone:	702-948-6937
Web:	www.eiffeltowerrestaurant.com
Prices:	$$$$

Lunch & dinner daily

Paris Las Vegas

Paris Las Vegas would be lacking if it didn't include a scale model of the Eiffel Tower. Like the original in France, this one has a pricey restaurant, too. To get there, take the glass elevator to the 11th floor of the replica *Tour Eiffel*. It's not the twinkling lights of Paris that you'll be looking down on through the floor-to-ceiling windows, but another city of lights: Las Vegas. Even so, this is a place to celebrate, be it with a significant other or a group.

As breathtaking as the views and décor are here, the French cuisine proves equally arresting. The menu, conceived by chef Jean Joho of Chicago's Everest, offers a multicourse prix-fixe option along with an à la carte selection that spotlights the likes of supreme of pheasant, and lobster Thermidor. For dessert, the ethereal soufflés will linger in your memory long after they've disappeared from your plate.

808 (Caesars Palace)

Hawaiian ✗✗

3570 Las Vegas Blvd. S.

Phone:	702-731-7731	Dinner daily
Web:	www.caesarspalace.com	
Prices:	**$$$**	

The Strip

©Mark Gibson

Say "aloha" to Hawaiian food at this elegant restaurant, just off the Palace Casino. Inspired by the cuisine of the Hawaiian Islands, where he worked for many years, French-born chef Jean-Marie Josselin introduces the flavors of the Pacific Rim to Caesars Palace. The name of his restaurant, which opened in 2000, echoes Hawaii's area code. Indeed, 808 just might be your lucky number if you favor Pacific fish such as sesame-crusted mahi mahi, grilled ono and seared hamachi.

Start your meal with one of the creative appetizers, perhaps seafood on ice, a deconstructed Ahi roll or a sampling of six appetizers in the New Wave Bento Box. Five-course chef's tasting menus offer both a seafood and a shellfish version.

Wave-shaped glass wall partitions, Asian lanterns, and a ceiling lined with stylized copper oyster shells bring a breezy island feel to the stylish dining room.

Emeril's (MGM Grand)

024

Seafood ✗✗

3799 Las Vegas Blvd. S.

Phone:	702-891-7374	Lunch & dinner daily
Web:	www.mgmgrand.com	
Prices:	$$$	

MGM Mirage

Emeril Lagasse arrived on the Vegas scene with his signature "Bam!" to kick up the MGM Grand with a bite of the Big Easy. One of the few restaurants in this hotel that is open for lunch, Emeril's offers three different seating areas: the oyster bar in the center of the room, the cafe near the entrance, and the dining room in back.

No matter where you sit, your taste buds will delight in seafood (note the deconstructed fish sculpture at the entrance) such as the signature New Orleans BBQ shrimp, served in a sauce fragrant with chile powder and cumin, with a tender, flaky rosemary biscuit alongside. Spices and flavors combine in unique ways in dishes such as blue crab cakes flecked with mild green chiles, or andouille-crusted redfish on a bed of creamy grits. If you still have room for dessert, Emeril's sinful banana cream pie will dash any hopes you had of dieting.

Empress Court (Caesars Palace)

The Strip

3570 Las Vegas Blvd. S.

Phone:	702-731-7731	Wed – Sun dinner only
Web:	www.caesarspalace.com	
Prices:	$$$	

Harrah's

Accessed via its own elevator (look for the two large bronze Chinese lions next to Rao's), Empress Court dramatically appears as a grand columned rotunda. It soars up to a night-sky ceiling studded with shining stars. From these heights, gauzy fabric panels cascade down into the center of a room filled with round tables topped with bowls of delicate orchids.

In this oasis of calm and luxury, well-trained servers elegantly present each dish to well-heeled connoisseurs of Cantonese cuisine. The extensive menu lists such unique ingredients as shark's fin, bird's nest, and abalone as separate categories, along with more usual fare. Two multicourse tastings—The Emperor and The Empress—expose the range of the chef's skills.

Dine on the terrace for a peek at the palm trees and classical architecture of the resort's 4.5-acre Garden of the Gods Pool.

Fiamma (MGM Grand)

3799 Las Vegas Blvd. S.

Phone:	702-891-7600	Dinner daily
Web:	www.mgmgrand.com	
Prices:	$$$	

The Strip

MGM Mirage

MGM Studio Walk is where you'll find the western cousin of SoHo's beloved Fiamma Osteria. Like its chic New York relative, this Fiamma specializes in soigné Italian dishes in which the different components deliciously complement the main ingredient without overpowering it. The likes of ravioli filled with short ribs braised in Barolo, and an antipasto of twisting ribbons of smoky-sweet prosciutto, cubes of aged Caciocavollo cheese, and briny Taggiasca olives will ignite your taste buds—an experience befitting a restaurant whose name means "flame" in Italian.

Fiamma in Las Vegas adopts a stylish but casual design in its 7,000-square-foot bi-level dining space. An open fireplace in the lounge and a sculptural "wave wall" suggesting desert dunes lend a sensuous quality, while a variety of wood surfaces reinforce the organic feel of the place.

51

Fin (Mirage)

Chinese ✗✗

027

3400 Las Vegas Blvd. S.

Phone:	702-791-7111	Lunch & dinner daily
Web:	www.mirage.com	
Prices:	$$	

MGM Mirage

There's something to be said for predictability. And when you're tired of guessing your odds at the casino, count on Fin to double down on familiar Chinese dishes.

Straightforward flavors brighten tried-and-true fare here. Tasty hot-and-sour soup, for instance, is made with white pepper to spice it up and vinegar to make it tangy; chicken *chow fun* blends chewy pan-fried noodles with a tender breast of chicken, all caramelized in salty soy sauce.

All this tradition plays successfully against striking contemporary décor: strings of smoky glass "pearls" hang like curtains from above, dividing the space into intimate smaller sections. Backlit illustrated panels along the walls diffuse the light in a room colored by chocolate-brown wood and accented by dark gray and ecru. The elegantly casual clientele counts conventioneers as well as Asian tourists among its numbers.

Fleur de Lys (Mandalay Bay)

Contemporary XXX

028

3950 Las Vegas Blvd. S.

Phone:	702-632-9400	Dinner daily
Web:	www.mandalaybay.com	
Prices:	$$$$	

MGM Mirage

In 2004 Alsatian-born chef Hubert Keller gambled on Mandalay Bay as a second location for a branch of his famed San Francisco restaurant. It seems he hit the jackpot with this soaring space, where a sand-colored stone wall holds a striking leaf-shaped frame filled with hundreds of fresh flower blossoms.

You'll have to choose between three different prix-fixe options, ranging from the basic (appetizer, entrée and dessert) to a five-course procession that adds a fish and a cheese course, as well as wine pairings for an extra fee. French regionals—including some rare offerings— lie at the heart of the wine list, which honors America with a good selection of California and Oregon labels.

While flickering candlelight casts an intimate glow on the closely spaced tables, several tented areas along the wall accommodate those who seek a private retreat.

Francesco's (Treasure Island)

Italian ✗✗

3300 Las Vegas Blvd. S.

Phone: 702-894-7348   Sat – Wed dinner only
Web: www.treasureisland.com
Prices: $$

MGM Mirage

Seek out Francesco's for a sojourn to the Italian countryside. Take a seat in the airy dining room, with its stone-washed walls, Venetian-style chandeliers, terra-cotta urns and bouquets of bright flowers, and imagine you're in a Tuscan villa. Ignore the clanging of the casino—which would surely not adjoin your haven in Tuscany—and give in to the casual atmosphere and the jovial and efficient service that feed the good times here.

Italian-American favorites—osso buco, grilled calamari, homemade gnocchi, risotto *del giorno*, and chicken papardelle in a creamy tomato sauce—appear on the table in hearty portions from the exhibition kitchen. You know you're in Vegas when you stop to consider that the creamy tiramisú accompanied by a strong shot of espresso should supply you with enough sugar and caffeine to keep you awake for hours of gaming and club-hopping to come.

Grand Lux Cafe (Venetian)

International ✕✕

3355 Las Vegas Blvd. S.

Phone:	702-414-3888	Lunch & dinner daily
Web:	www.grandluxcafe.com	
Prices:	$$	

Grand Lux Cafe

No place illustrates the axiom that "more is more" better than Las Vegas, and this capacious cafe in the Venetian—which can accommodate more than 500 guests—is no exception.

Families and large groups flock to the decorous dining space for its international menu, sharing-sized portions and moderate prices. Designed to please a range of eclectic palates, offerings here run the gamut from Yankee pot roast and Cajun shrimp to Southeast Asian shaking beef and Italian-inspired pastas. Confections such as banana cream pie, strawberry shortcake and warm apple crisp are made fresh in the on-site bakery; cheesecakes come courtesy of the cafe's sister restaurant, The Cheesecake Factory. If you're in a hurry, you can place your order to go.

Located on the ground-floor casino level, the Grand Lux stays open 24/7 and serves breakfast, lunch and dinner.

The Strip

Grand Wok & Sushi Bar
(MGM Grand)

031

Asian

3799 Las Vegas Blvd. S.

Phone: 800-929-1111
Web: www.mgmgrand.com
Prices: $$

Lunch & dinner daily

MGM Mirage

Slightly elevated off the MGM Grand casino floor, the Grand Wok's entrance is designated by blond wood, black granite accents and a bubbling water feature. Inside the sleek space, thick glass panels shield the dining room from the cacophony of the slot machines while offering views of all the action.

Taking its cues from China, Japan, Thailand, Korea, Vietnam and Malaysia, the cuisine at Grand Wok features Asian dishes from spicy Kung Pao chicken and seafood clay pot to sushi rolls and fragrant Thai noodle soup. Fresh ingredients yield flavorful food, served in portions large enough to satisfy the most robust appetites.

One caveat: the Grand Wok is open for lunch and dinner, but if it's sushi or sashimi you crave, you'll have to wait until dinnertime since the sushi bar is only open in the evening.

Guy Savoy ✿✿ (Caesars Palace)

French ✗✗✗✗

3570 Las Vegas Blvd. S.

Phone: 702-731-7286   Wed – Sun dinner only
Web: www.guysavoy.com
Prices: $$$$

The Strip

Caesars Palace

On the Vegas Strip, nobody likes to be outdone. So, to maintain its epicurean reputation, Caesars Palace recently imported stellar French chef Guy Savoy to the second floor of the Augustus Tower. This exclusive restaurant emulates its three-star sibling in Paris; both are designed with Zen-like minimalism by renowned architect Jean-Michel Wilmotte. Cathedral-high ceilings, carved wood panels, leather and stone accents, and serene lighting harmonize perfectly in this temple of gastronomy.

Guy Savoy also recalls the chef's Paris flagship in its artful menu, transforming magnificent ingredients into signatures such as the rich artichoke and black truffle soup and the ethereal *côte de gros turbot*. Behind the glass wine wall, 1,000 bottles of predominantly French wine recite the best of Burgundy and Bordeaux, as well as more affordable varietals from the Loire and Rhone valleys.

Appetizers	*Entrées*	*Desserts*
● Colors of Caviar	● Crispy Sea Bass and Delicate Spices	● Grapefruit Terrine, Earl Grey Tea Sauce
● Artichoke and Black Truffle Soup	● Roasted Veal Chop, Vegetables of Season and Black Truffle Potato Purée	● Chocolate Fondant, Crunchy Praline and Chicory Cream
● Oysters in Ice Gelée	● American Prime Beef Tenderloin and Paleron à la Française	● Dessert Trolley with Ice Creams, Sorbets and Traditional French Pastries

Hyakumi (Caesars Palace)

The Strip

Japanese

3570 Las Vegas Blvd. S.

Phone: 702-731-7731   Lunch & dinner daily
Web: www.caesarspalace.com
Prices: $$$

Harrah's

Facing the floating lounge called Cleopatra's Barge, Hyakumi (pronounced ya COO me) bids you to find respite from the boisterous casino in its placid sushi bar, which evokes a Japanese tea-garden vibe with bamboo screens and waitresses clad in kimonos.

If you're doing well at the tables, sample some sushi, and try one of the interesting combination dinners, served with miso soup, rice and tempura. Then perhaps treat your friends to a bottle of premium sake. If you're down on your luck, note that ordering à la carte can add up quickly; a better option might be the inexpensive noodle dishes.

A room at the back of the restaurant is dedicated to *teppan yaki* cuisine (available only at dinner). Here, tables come equipped with iron griddles on which you can cook your own choice of ingredients from tiger shrimp to Kobe beef.

Il Mulino (Caesars Palace)

034

The Forum Shops, 3500 Las Vegas Blvd. S.

Phone: 702-492-6000
Web: www.ilmulinonewyork.com
Prices: $$$$

Mon – Sat lunch & dinner
Sun dinner only

The Strip

Il Mulino

This Greenwich Village stalwart recently headed west with a satellite at Caesars Palace. Located on the third and top level of the labyrinthine Forum Shops, Il Mulino continues the tradition started more than 20 years ago by brothers Fernando and Gino Masci in New York City.

A meal here will set you back a few bucks, but for your money you'll be treated to Old World slow-cooked food, served in a refined ambience adorned with wrought-iron chandeliers, a claret-colored carpet, and a display of mouth-watering products against one wall. Imported cheeses, olive oils and salamis complement a menu that highlights the bold flavors of the Abruzzi region, home to the brothers Masci. If you couldn't tear yourself away from the slots long enough to have lunch, you'll appreciate the big portions.

Try for a table on the pleasant indoor terrace.

Isla (Treasure Island)

Mexican ✗✗

3300 Las Vegas Blvd. S.

Phone: 702-894-7349   Dinner daily
Web: www.treasureisland.com
Prices: $$

MGM Mirage

Park your pirate ship outside and swagger on in to Isla. With lively Latin music, young, friendly servers, and a menu created by Mexican-born chef Richard Sandoval (of Pampano and Maya in New York City), Isla whips up good food and fun at Treasure Island. Enter through the tequila bar, where premium tequila is the quaff of choice—mixed into margaritas or enjoyed in a Goddess Elixir, prepared tableside by Isla's own sensual Tequila Goddess.

Don't get hung up at the bar, though, or you'll miss the main attraction: traditional Mexican dishes with a sexy modern twist. Several different types of guacamole are prepared tableside; grilled filet mignon comes with a cheese enchilada in mole sauce; and the chile relleno is presented in a luscious tomato broth with beef picadillo and Oaxaca cheese served alongside (instead of being stuffed into) the chile.

Joël Robuchon ✿✿✿ (MGM Grand)

Contemporary 🍴🍴🍴🍴

3799 Las Vegas Blvd. S.

Phone: 702-891-7925
Web: www.mgmgrand.com
Prices: $$$$

Dinner daily

The Strip

MGM Mirage

Fashioned as an opulent Belle Époque salon, down to the last ornate wall molding, this restaurant feels miles away from the casino just outside the doors. Settle into a purple velvet banquette or a table in the landscaped indoor garden, and the world simply melts away.

Prepare to experience perfection on a plate. Celebrated chef Joël Robuchon, who came out of retirement a few years ago, is now an integral part of the Vegas fine-dining arena. Presented with striking visual effect, his transcendent dishes (as in pan-seared sea bass with lemongrass foam or truffle velouté on celeriac custard with sweet onion) find inspiration throughout the regions of France.

A meal here is an event, during which you'll progress through a series of courses (your choice between two tasting menus), beginning with a tableau of artisan breads and ending with a palette of jewel-like miniature pastries, jellies and chocolates.

Appetizers

- Crispy Soft-boiled Egg with Smoked Salmon and Osetra Caviar
- Layer of Fresh Tomato and King Crab with Coulis Verjuté
- Truffled Langoustine Ravioli with Chopped Cabbage

Entrées

- French Hen (for 2) with Roasted Foie Gras, Braised Potatoes
- Sautéed Veal Chop, Herb Jus, Vegetable Mille-Feuille
- Sea Bass with Lemongrass Foam, Stewed Baby Leeks

Desserts

- Pink Grapefruit with Violets, Lychee Sorbet
- Warm Soufflé Perfumed with Yuzu and Banana Ice Cream
- Crunchy Pearls of Manjari, Mint Ice Cream

61

Joe's (Caesars Palace)

037

The Forum Shops, 3500 Las Vegas Blvd. S.

Phone: 702-792-9222   Lunch & dinner daily
Web: www.icon.com/joes
Prices: $$

Joe's Seafood, Prime Steak and Stone Crab

A Miami icon, Joe's has long been a must-stop on any diner's tour of South Beach. Famous for their stone-crab claws, Joe's has been in business since 1913 when Joe Weiss set up a little lunch counter on Miami Beach. In 2004 Joe's opened in the Forum Shops, to the delight of stone-crab lovers in the desert.

Seafood (scallops, shrimp and fresh fish flown in from around the world) is the best reason to dine here, though the restaurant does offer a fine selection of prime steaks and chops, too. But you'll regret it later if you don't try the stone crabs, served chilled with the creamy house mustard sauce. For dessert, savor a slice of Key lime pie and dream of balmy afternoons in South Beach.

The indoor terrace facing the fountain and statuary in the ground-level atrium makes a grand spot in which to sip a glass of wine from the extensive list of American labels.

L'Atelier de Joël Robuchon ✥
(MGM Grand)

Contemporary ✗✗

038

3799 Las Vegas Blvd. S.

Phone: 702-891-7358   Dinner daily
Web: www.mgmgrand.com
Prices: $$$$

MGM Mirage

Styled after Joël Robuchon's renowned Parisian original, L'Atelier is in every sense a studio. Most of the seats range around the black granite counter that faces the open kitchen. From here you can watch as meticulous chefs paint plates with stripes of sauce, carve paper-thin slices of *jamon Iberico*, or fill miniature cast-iron cocottes with Robuchon's sinfully rich (and worth every last calorie!) *pommes purée*. Select as many small plates as you like from the extensive dégustation menu, or choose main-course items à la carte. For those who choose not to choose, there's a set tasting menu too.

Food doubles as still life in the black and red room: bowls of ripe tomatoes and displays of fresh baby greens might serve as centerpieces on the counter, while flawless fruits, jars of preserved peppers and flats of eggs are artfully arranged in the glassed-in storage area.

Appetizers	*Entrées*	*Desserts*
• Crispy Langoustine Fritter with Basil Pesto	• Free-range Quail Stuffed with Foie Gras with Truffled Mashed Potatoes	• Chartreuse Soufflé, Pistachio Ice Cream
• Mediterranean Vegetables Layered with Buffalo Mozzarella	• Fresh Cod Filet in a Vegetable Broth	• Chocolate Sensation, Crémeux Araguani, Oreo Cookie Crumbs
• Poached Baby Kussi Oysters with Echiré Butter	• Sweetbreads with Fresh Laurel and Stuffed Romaine Lettuce	• Raspberry Surprise inside White Chocolate Sphere, Yuzu Ice Cream

Le Cirque ✿ (Bellagio)

French 🍴🍴🍴

3600 Las Vegas Blvd. S.

Dinner daily

Phone: 702-693-8100
Web: www.bellagio.com
Prices: $$$$

MGM Mirage

Le Cirque ringmaster Sirio Maccioni took his show on the road when he opened the Las Vegas outpost of his storied New York City restaurant. On the perimeter of Bellagio's casino, Le Cirque brings Adam Tihany's conception of a sophisticated circus to life. Step right up and admire the multicolored backlit silk canopy, which drapes like a tent over the room. Circus scenes decorate three walls, while the fourth is lined with windows overlooking another spectacle—Bellagio's fountain and light show.

The kitchen performs impressive culinary feats with the greatest of ease, crafting imaginative dishes from irreproachably fresh products and classic French recipes (the signature roast chicken, for example, is served with earthy black truffles stuffed under its skin).

This is a place to get dolled up; most guests adhere to the suggested dress code (jackets for gentlemen).

Appetizers	*Entrées*	*Desserts*
• Diver Scallops, Langoustine en Kadaif, Mosaic of Beets	• Honey-glazed Duck with Fig, Daikon and Black Currant	• Warm Chocolate Fondant, Caramelized Bananas, Tahitian Vanilla Ice Cream
• Lobster Salad "Le Cirque"	• Organic Roasted Chicken with Summer White Truffle and Porcini	• Baba au Rum, Strawberry Soup, Coconut Ice Cream
• Terrine of Foie Gras, Seasonal Fruits and Grapes Chutney, "Gewürztraminer" Jelly		

Mesa Grill ✿ (Caesars Palace)

040

3570 Las Vegas Blvd. S.

Phone:	702-731-7731	Lunch & dinner daily
Web:	www.mesagrill.com	
Prices:	$$$	

The Strip

©Gary Moss / Mesa Grill

Shake up bold flavors, primary colors and a casino just adjacent, and you've got Bobby Flay in Vegas. The Caesars Palace incarnation of the chef's popular New York City grill separates itself from the gaming tables by walls of tinted glass, leaving the focus clearly on the display kitchen—and the sophisticated food.

Tastes of the Southwest come with a lively Mexican touch here in spicy chicken and sweet-potato hash topped with poached eggs and green-chile hollandaise, or a zesty blackened Florida grouper in sour-orange sauce, served with a side of oregano spoonbread. Careful not to overwhelm the main ingredients, the kitchen staff perks up dishes with the assertive use of chile peppers, cilantro and garlic, producing a rich harmony of flavors.

Tequila aficionados can add a "Smoky Floater" of Del Maguey "Chichicapa" single-village mescal to any margarita.

Appetizers	*Entrées*	*Desserts*
• Barbecued Duck Blue Corn Pancake	• Ancho Chile Honey-glazed Salmon	• Warm Chocolate Cake
• Shrimp and Grouper Ceviche	• New Mexican Spice-rubbed Pork Tenderloin	• Smoked Vanilla Toasted Walnut Flan
• Tiger Shrimp and Roast Garlic Corn Tamale	• Grilled Mahi Mahi	• Milk Chocolate Espresso Tart

Michael Mina ✿ (Bellagio)

Contemporary 🍴🍴🍴

3600 Las Vegas Blvd. S.

Phone:	702-693-8199	Dinner daily
Web:	www.bellagio.com	
Prices:	$$$$	

MGM Mirage

Bet on award-winning chef Michael Mina (known for his eponymous restaurant in San Francisco) to bring his unique take on seafood to the desert. There may be nary an ocean nearby, but at Mina's Bellagio outpost, fabulously fresh fish (raw hamachi coated in a creamy aïoli infused with ginger, garlic and scallions; black-truffle-studded lobster potpie served tableside from the copper pot it was cooked in) swim away with the accolades. For dessert, the chef's twist on a classic root-beer float, served in an old-fashioned soda glass with two dark-chocolate straws, will make you feel like a kid again.

To find the restaurant, walk beyond Bellagio's lobby through the Conservatory, full of stunning floral displays. In the restaurant, Tony Chi's soothing design incorporates an exhibition kitchen that runs the length of the dining room; windows offer views of Bellagio's manicured pool area.

Appetizers

- Trio of Seared Diver Scallops
- Trio of American Kobe-Style Beef Carpaccio
- Savory Mussel Soufflé with Saffron-Chardonnay Cream

Entrées

- Trio of Olive Oil-poached Lamb
- Trio of Potato-crusted John Dory
- Medallions of Ahi Tuna with Seared Hudson Valley Foie Gras

Desserts

- Old-Fashioned Root Beer Float with Warm Chocolate Chip Pecan Cookies
- Banana Bomb, Coconut Dacquoise, Milk Chocolate Ice Cream, Caramel-Rum Sauce

miX ❀ (Mandalay Bay)

042

3950 Las Vegas Blvd. S.

Dinner daily

Phone: 702-632-9500
Web: www.chinagrillmgt.com
Prices: $$$$

The Strip

MGM Mirage

In a city where every opulent detail vies for your attention, miX will steal your breath away. Looking down on The Strip from its 64th-floor aerie in THEhotel, Alain Ducasse's Vegas venture dazzles with a futuristic design conceived by Patrick Jouin. Curving lines and iridescent pearl tones shimmer beneath stunning strands of hand-blown Murano glass bubbles—15,000 in all—that cascade down from the ceiling. The best seat in the house is on the heated terrace; beneath you The Strip spreads out in all its neon splendor. A meal here unfolds like a perfectly choreographed ballet, during which the corps of gracious servers never misses a step. First on stage might be a cylinder of spicy crab salad crowned with a julienne of green papaya and mango; next up, perhaps a *pas de deux* of pepper tuna two ways. Finales like the tea-infused chocolate tart merit a standing ovation.

Appetizers

- Tender Potato Gnocchi, Asparagus, Wild Mushroom and Parmigiano
- Lobster Salad, Avocado, Tomato Confit, Caviar Cream
- Duck Foie Gras Terrine, Pineapple Chutney

Entrées

- Sautéed Scallops, Endive, Cilantro/ Citrus Emulsion
- Roasted Maine Lobster "au Curry", Coconut Basmati Rice
- Bison Tenderloin, "Sauce au Poivre", Mix of Vegetables

Desserts

- miX Candy Bar
- Rhubarb Strawberry, Crispy Coconut Cream, Pineapple Sorbet
- Chocolate/Coffee Martini Espresso

Mon Ami Gabi (Paris)

043

French XX

3655 Las Vegas Blvd. S.

Phone:	702-944-4224	Lunch & dinner daily
Web:	www.parislasvegas.com	
Prices:	$$	

The Strip

Paris Las Vegas

One of the few restaurants that offers an open-air terrace on The Strip, Mon Ami Gabi makes a great place for people-watching (complete with misters to cool patrons during the searing desert summers). The patio, nestled under the Eiffel Tower at Paris Las Vegas, is also a great dining spot, complete with a view of the Bellagio fountain show, which takes place right across the street.

Inside, Belle Époque style abounds in the authentically re-created bistro named for owner and chef Gabino Sotelino. Steak is the specialty of Mon Ami Gabi, which bills itself as a French steakhouse. However, the menu goes well beyond steak, with the likes of roast chicken, trout Grenobloise, and mussels with *frites* sharing billing with grilled salmon salad, burgers and a duck BLT. Wines by the glass are served in style from a rolling cart.

Nobhill (MGM Grand)

Californian 🍴🍴🍴

3799 Las Vegas Blvd. S.

Phone: 702-891-7337
Web: www.michaelmina.net
Prices: $$$$

Dinner dinner

The Strip

MGM Mirage

Named for a ritzy and historic section of San Francisco, Nobhill embodies Michael Mina's idea of an urban neighborhood restaurant. In this case, though, the neighborhood is The Strip, and the décor downplays Vegas glitz for a sleek and sophisticated look, warmed by tones of chocolate brown and creamy beige.

Despite Nobhill's location, many of the restaurant's dishes (North Beach cioppino, whole fried Sonoma chicken tetrazzini, Dungeness crab Louie) draw their inspiration and their ingredients from the Bay Area. And Michael Mina fans will be glad to know that the menu includes the chef's signature Maine lobster potpie. If you want to make an evening of it, go for one of the tasting menus (available for the entire table only).

Listing libations like the Cable Car, Mission Margarita, and Potrero Fizz, the cocktail menu leaves its heart in San Francisco.

Noodles (Bellagio)

Asian 🍴

3600 Las Vegas Blvd. S.

Phone: 702-693-7111   Lunch & dinner daily
Web: www.bellagio.com
Prices: 💰

The Strip

MGM Mirage

You'll find this little Asian eatery hidden behind a bank of slot machines next to the Salon Privé and the Baccarat room. No secret anymore, Noodles is well worth seeking out for its inexpensive Far East fare, which employs top-quality products.

Marble floors and a backlit display of apothecary jars filled with different types of—you guessed it—noodles highlight the décor, while the menu takes inspiration from different parts of Asia. Signatures such as roasted soya chicken (made with "ancient" soy sauce), vermicelli with pork knuckle, and premier fried rice with pineapple, sausage, pork floss, raisins and shrimp number among the long list of tasty dishes. Sure bets are the spicy noodle soups, or the wok-fried noodle entrées.

Those looking for small bites will want to go for dim sum, served Friday to Sunday from 11am to 3pm.

The Noodle Shop (Mandalay Bay)

046

A s i a n ✗

3950 Las Vegas Blvd. S.

Phone:	702-632-7800	Lunch & dinner daily
Web:	www.mandalaybay.com	
Prices:	**$$**	

© Mark Gibson

Looking for a place to lunch in Mandalay Bay? Oodles of noodles are what you'll find at The Noodle Shop. Bold flavors and high-quality ingredients composing the Asian cuisine here will please your palate, while copious portions of dishes like chicken pad Thai, noodle soups, Cantonese beef stew, and Thousand Year egg and shredded pork congee will fill you up so you can spend more uninterrupted hours at the casino.

The recently renovated Asian cafe sports a sleek, contemporary design that stands in sharp contrast to its traditional menu. Speedy, friendly service and proximity to the hotel's convention center make this place a good bet for a casual midday meal in between business meetings—especially since it's one of the few restaurants in Mandalay Bay that is open for lunch. Perhaps best of all, it won't cost all your winnings to eat here.

Okada (Wynn)

Japanese XXX

3131 Las Vegas Blvd. S.

Phone:	702-248-3463	Dinner daily
Web:	www.wynnlasvegas.com	
Prices:	$$$	

The Strip

Wynn Las Vegas

Steve Wynn isn't bashful when it comes to the names in his hotel. Thus it's no surprise that this elegant Japanese restaurant takes its title from a friend of Wynn's who is also an investor in the resort.

Okada's food wanders the world of Japanese cuisine from sushi and sashimi to *robatayaki* to hot (braised Kurobuta short rib) and cold (chilled seared bigeye tuna) plates. Offerings such as Iranian Osetra caviar and seared foie gras take the menu well beyond the standard sushi bar, and a separate space devoted to *teppan yaki* dining is equipped with heated cooktops. Sake is the drink of choice, with a host of bottles artfully displayed behind the bar.

Pendulous moon-like Japanese lanterns, a floating pagoda table, and what looks like a web of giant black chopsticks lining the ceiling compose a contemporary dining landscape that refers to Japan's rich history.

Olives (Bellagio)

048

3600 Las Vegas Blvd. S.

Phone: 702-693-8255
Web: www.bellagio.com
Prices: $$$

Lunch & dinner daily

The Strip

Olives

A concept started by chef Todd English in Charlestown, Massachusetts in 1989, Olives now claims multiple locations across the U.S. Mediterranean cuisine is the name of the game here, and English plays it well. The duo of green and black olive tapenade that is delivered to your table along with crusty Italian bread echoes the restaurant's name and creates a good first impression of what is to come. Flatbread pizzas and house-made pastas make a fitting prelude to brick-oven-roasted chicken, veal osso buco, and grilled fish.

The restaurant, which incorporates an organic décor colored by browns and greens, and a striking mosaic tile floor, occupies a spot next to Hermès in the Via Bellagio shopping arcade. When the weather's not too sweltering, a table on the terrace overlooking Lake Bellagio and the resort's famed fountains is de rigueur.

Orchid (Venetian)

049

3355 Las Vegas Blvd. S.

Phone: 702-414-2220   Dinner daily
Web: www.venetian.com
Prices: **$$$**

The Venetian

Refined and delicate as the flower from which the restaurant borrows its name, the Chinese cuisine at Orchid encompasses a wide range of dishes and prices.

Chef Simon To, a native of Hong Kong, specializes in Canton and Szechwan styles of cooking. Thus, there are scallops with asparagus in XO sauce, Hong Kong-style seafood pan-fried noodles, and Szechwan hot-and-sour soup. But that's not all. Dim sum and rolls, congee noodles and rice, stir-fried vegetables, and live seafood are just a few of the extensive menu choices. Among the more expensive and prized dishes, you'll find braised shark-fin soup with crabmeat, and braised abalone with seasonal vegetables. Located on the casino floor of The Venetian, Orchid is a serene oasis decked out with minimalist contemporary décor, soothed by Asian music, and attended to by a polite and discreet waitstaff.

Osteria Del Circo (Bellagio)

Italian

050

3600 Las Vegas Blvd. S.

Phone: 702-693-8150
Web: www.osteriadelcirco.com
Prices: $$$$

Dinner daily

MGM Mirage

Standing shoulder to shoulder with older sibling Le Cirque, this lighthearted osteria dazzles with blazing burgundy and gold hues and a big-top theme conceived by Adam Tihany. The menu proposes a balanced array of clay-oven-baked pizzas, house-made pastas (the sheep's-milk ricotta ravioli in sage butter sauce comes highly recommended), fish and meat dishes. On the wine list, you'll discover some fine Barolos and Barbarescos schmoozing with an A-list of California labels. Service is sophisticated and surprisingly formal, so if you're looking for a casual atmosphere, camp out at the lively bar.

This restaurant used to be the lower-priced alternative to Le Cirque, but a recent price hike kicked up the cost of a meal here (i.e., $19 for a thin-crust pizza) closer to the range of its uptown sister next door.

P.F. Chang's (Planet Hollywood)

051 | Chinese ✗✗

3667 Las Vegas Blvd. S.

Phone: 702-836-0955
Web: www.pfchangs.com
Prices: $$

Lunch & dinner daily

&

🕐

P.F. Chang's Chinese Bistro

Those who have dined in P.F. Chang's in other cities—the chain reaches from coast to coast—will recognize the life-size replicas of ancient Terra-Cotta Army statues that greet visitors to this satellite in Planet Hollywood's casino. (The original army of clay horses and soldiers was commissioned by China's first emperor, Qin Shi Huang, to guard him in the afterlife.)

Concentrating on Mandarin-style wok cooking, chefs in the exhibition kitchen prepare updated versions of reasonably priced Chinese standards. Vegetarian lettuce wraps, harvest spring rolls and steamed or pan-fried dumplings come with the freshest of vegetables, and share menu space with a wide range of traditional dishes from lo mein to twice-cooked beef à la Sichuan. In case you were wondering, entrepreneur Paul Fleming (of Ruth's Chris and Fleming's Prime steakhouse chains) is the "P.F." in the name.

Pampas (Planet Hollywood)

Brazilian ✗✗

Miracle Mile Shops, 3663 Las Vegas Blvd. S.

Lunch & dinner daily

Phone:	702-737-4748
Web:	www.pampasusa.com
Prices:	$$

©Steve Spatafore/ Pampas Churrascaria

The Strip

Wrangle a bunch of buddies and make way to Planet Hollywood's Miracle Mile Shops; if you've got a big appetite, you'll get a good deal here. Evoking the *churrasco*-style of eating that evolved on the high plains of southern Brazil, Pampas spit-roasts cuts of meat from chicken breasts to Brazilian sausage to sirloin and delivers them on skewers to your table where they are carved at your request. Turn the disk on your table green-side-up to signal that you want more. Had enough? Flip your disk to red. Think of it as an epicurean version of the children's game Red Light, Green Light.

A range of vegetables, cold salads and cheeses are set up on the salad bar, and cheese bread and fried banana and chickpea fritters are served to each table. You can choose a wine from the list that comes wrapped around a magnum bottle, or go for the gusto with a Brazilian cocktail.

Pearl (MGM Grand)

Chinese XXX

3799 Las Vegas Blvd. S.

Phone: 702-891-7380
Web: www.mgmgrand.com
Prices: $$$$

Dinner daily

The Strip

MGM Mirage

Obscured by a panel of frosted glass, Pearl is discreetly cached away from the main casino floor along MGM Grand's Studio Walk. Well-dressed couples and business diners favor this elegant restaurant, outfitted by New York designer Tony Chi with bold red lamps, dark wood furnishings and teal enamel accent tiles. High-backed cream suede booths along the wall provide the most intimate seating option.

Upscale Chinese cuisine here spotlights premium ingredients, with a focus on live seafood. Dishes from the changing seasonal menu (think crispy salt and pepper squid, steamed live garlic shrimp, fire-roasted Mongolian beef) are plated with artistic flair and presented with a formal flourish.

A pot of fresh-brewed tea is the traditional way to end a meal at this gem of a restaurant; once on the table, the teapot keeps warm over a votive oil lamp.

Picasso ✿✿ (Bellagio)

054

3600 Las Vegas Blvd. S.

Phone:	702-693-7223	Wed – Mon dinner only
Web:	www.bellagio.com	
Prices:	$$$$	

The Strip

MGM Mirage

Take the name literally. Set about with original paintings and ceramics by the restaurant's namesake artist, as well as stylish carpeting and furniture designed by Pablo's son, Claude, Picasso gives a whole new meaning to the art of dining. While the dining room's floor-to-ceiling windows look out at more than 1,000 fountains that perform a dazzling spectacle of water and light at regular intervals, the view can't begin to compete with the stunning—and priceless—artwork inside.

Spanish-born chef Julian Serrano, who has been the master of Picasso's kitchen since it opened in 1998, paints his epicurean canvas with broad, well-executed strokes. Flavors of Spain and France (where Picasso spent much of his life) color the cuisine in two different tasting menus featuring thoughtfully composed dishes and exquisite presentations. The global wine list overflows with fine French labels.

Appetizers

- Quail Salad with Artichokes, Pine Nuts and Truffle Vinaigrette
- Scallop with Asparagus and Hollandaise Mousseline
- Foie Gras with Cherries, Port Orange Zest and Walnut Crust

Entrées

- Medallions of Fallow Deer with Caramelized Green Apples
- Roasted Milk-fed Veal Chop with Confit of Rosemary Potatoes

Desserts

- Apple Tasting: Strudel, Napoleon, Ice Cream
- Vanilla Crêpes: Strawberry Compote, Cream Cheese Muscat Sorbet
- Tasting of Berries: Cheesecake, Dacquoise, Soup

Pinot Brasserie (Venetian)

French ✗✗

3355 Las Vegas Blvd. S.

Phone: 702-414-8888
Web: www.patinagroup.com
Prices: $$$

Lunch & dinner daily

Pinot Brasserie

Open for breakfast, lunch and dinner, this Gallic brasserie in the Venetian is decked out à la mode with antiques imported from France, red-leather banquettes and honey-toned wood paneling. While the titles of the dishes are in French, and tasty fare *(moules marinière, steak frites, magret de canard)* dominates the choices, the menu speaks in American accents when it mentions the likes of steak and eggs for breakfast, a lobster club sandwich or the multicultural hamburger for lunch, and a Caesar salad and a bone-in ribeye "cowboy" steak for dinner.

No matter what accent you speak in, join the crowd of conventioneers and visitors who find that this member of chef Joachim Splichal's Patina Restaurant Group makes an equally convenient place for a meal between meetings or before a show.

The Strip

Postrio (Venetian)

Contemporary ✕✕✕

3355 Las Vegas Blvd. S.

Phone: 702-796-1110

Web: www.wolfgangpuck.com

Prices: $$$

Lunch & dinner daily

The Strip

The Wolfgang Puck Fine Dining Group

If you've come to Vegas with your heart set on shopping, Postrio, bordering the re-creation of St. Mark's Square in the Grand Canal Shoppes, is ideally situated for a lunch break. Lunch at the cafe features a menu of salads, pastas and wood-oven-baked pizzas, as well as pork Wiener Schnitzel and other favorites of Austrian chef and owner Wolfgang Puck. Terrace seating under the artificial sky generates a sunny ambience all year round, no matter the weather outside.

In the evening, this star in Puck's constellation of Vegas restaurants opens its classy, upscale dining room where civility and comfort rule in an Old World climate fostered by jewel tones and blown-glass chandeliers. Like big sister Postrio in San Francisco, changing entrées here (Peking-style roasted duck, braised beef short-rib gnocchi) exhibit a global flair.

Prime Steakhouse (Bellagio)

Steakhouse ✗✗✗

3600 Las Vegas Blvd. S.

Phone: 702-693-7111
Web: www.bellagio.com
Prices: $$$$

Dinner daily

The Strip

MGM Mirage

You expect high glamour from a chophouse on the Las Vegas Strip, but even so, Jean-Georges Vongerichten's lakeside version in Bellagio surprises with its lavish décor. Inspired by a 1930s-era speakeasy, Prime dons pale blue marble for its floor, sumptuous blue velvet to frame the opening to its rooms, and Baccarat crystal to add sparkle to its chandelier. Table settings are equally well outfitted, complete with soft lighting suited to romance.

Top-quality meat dresses to impress in the likes of prime filet mignon, double-cut lamb chops and live Maine lobster. California's finest Cabernets, Merlots and Pinot Noirs strut their stuff on the wine list, along with an excellent selection of French Bordeaux.

For an after-dinner drink or a cigar, the outdoor terrace facing the dancing fountains can't be beat.

Rao's (Caesars Palace)

Italian ✗✗

058

3570 Las Vegas Blvd. S.

Phone: 877-346-4642
Web: www.raos.com
Prices: $$$

Wed – Sun lunch & dinner
Mon – Tue dinner only

©Barry Johnson/Harrah's

If Horatio Alger had lived a few years longer and moved to New York City, he could have used Rao's as a shining illustration in his rags-to-riches stories. Founded in East Harlem in 1896 by a family of Italian immigrants, this neighborhood red-sauce joint caught the attention of New York's culinary cognoscenti in 1977 when the New York Times gave it a rave review. Since then, the 10-table restaurant has been one of the city's hardest reservations to snag.

At its new branch in Caesars Palace, Rao's replicates the Harlem original on a larger scale. The smooth stylings of Martin and Sinatra provide background music as guests dig into big plates of rigatoni, lemon chicken and other family recipes. Rao's justly famous meatballs come as a *contorno* (side dish), served in tomato sauce and liberally dusted with parmesan. Backers are betting that Rao's will win big in Vegas.

Red 8 (Wynn)

059

Chinese ✗✗

3131 Las Vegas Blvd. S.

Phone: 702-248-3463
Web: www.wynnlasvegas.com
Prices: $$

Lunch & dinner daily

Red 8

Think you need to hit it big at the roulette table to eat in Steve Wynn's over-the-top hotel? Think again. Just a toss of the dice from the main casino floor, Red 8 provides a good and less expensive dining option in the chi-chi Wynn Las Vegas.

Not as formal as its neighbor Wing Lei, located down the corridor, this restaurant with its red and black motif opens for lunch, dinner, and late-night dining on weekends (Friday and Saturday until 1am). On the menu you'll find all the Chinese favorites (Kung Pao chicken, Mongolian beef, Szechwan shrimp), along with options from noodle dishes in broth to steamed live crab.

If you're feeling adventurous, gamble on more unique fare like jellyfish salad or braised abalone. In fact, there are so many items on the lengthy menu that you might be hard-pressed to choose—your decision could come down to, say, the spin of a wheel.

rm seafood (Mandalay Bay)

Seafood XXX

Mandalay Place, 3930 Las Vegas Blvd. S.

Phone: 702-632-9300
Web: www.rmseafood.com
Prices: $$$$

Lunch & dinner daily

The Strip

MGM Mirage

Expertly prepared, top-quality seafood steals the show at chef Rick Moonen's Vegas venture. Located at the entrance to Mandalay Place shopping area, sleek rm seafood occupies the second-level space, upstairs from the casual rbar cafe.

Sustainable seafood is the name of the game here, and all the fish on rm's menu are caught or farmed in environmentally friendly ways. Depending on the market, denizens of the deep might include moist, fork-tender Arctic char, pink prawns perched artistically on a stack of roasted squid, or diver scallops served with littleneck-clam risotto. Banquettes along both walls cosset couples, while stand-alone tables accommodate larger groups in the center of the intimate dining room. Downstairs, rbar dishes up bowls of clam chowder, platters of shellfish and more in a laid-back atmosphere animated by three large plasma-screen TVs.

rumjungle (Mandalay Bay)

061

Caribbean ✗✗

3950 Las Vegas Blvd. S.

Phone: 702-632-7408
Web: www.chinagrillmgt.com
Prices: $$$

Lunch & dinner daily

rumjungle

From the glowing, 144-foot-long rum bar to the booming music, this place clearly styles itself as a nightclub. But if you make your way through the entrance wall of flickering flames and past the stylish club-hopping crowd to the main dining area, you'll be rewarded with a tropical treat. Island ingredients form the centerpiece of flavorful entrées like Caribbean curried jambalaya shrimp, grilled sugarcane prawn salad with strawberry-papaya salsa, and rotisserie-roasted garlic-lime chicken with sweet coconut rice—not to mention meat and fish roasted over the open fire pit.

It's not only the food that's noteworthy. Jeffrey Beers' splashy décor in the three-tiered dining room is another feast for the senses with its zebra-striped tables, neon spotlights, and gigantic conga drums that rise from the floor each evening as the restaurant morphs into a pulsating nightspot.

SeaBlue (MGM Grand)

Seafood ✗✗

3799 Las Vegas Blvd. S.

Dinner daily

Phone: 702-891-3486
Web: www.michaelmina.net
Prices: $$$$

MGM Mirage

The Strip

Michael Mina's contemporary seafood-centric brasserie hooks the fruits of the sea, flown in fresh daily. The cuisine of the Mediterranean and North Africa inspires dishes such as a whole wood-grilled *loup de mer* accompanied by rice studded with earthy brown lentils and topped with buttery chickpeas, or tandoori octopus with crunchy tabbouleh and turmeric sambal. Versions of all-American state-fair favorites make waves too, as the kitchen whips up whimsical deep-fried lobster corn dogs served with pungent whole-grain mustard.

Check out the chefs as they craft your meal in the open kitchen and at the two food-preparation areas located on one side of the three-sided bar in the middle of the room. Famed restaurant designer Adam Tihany has outfitted SeaBlue's space with polished brick floors, vibrant red lantern-like light fixtures, and streaming water walls.

Sensi (Bellagio)

Contemporary ✗✗

3600 Las Vegas Blvd. S.

Phone: 702-693-8800
Web: www.bellagio.com
Prices: $$

Lunch & dinner daily

MGM Mirage

Modern and minimalist, Sensi titillates your senses with rushing waterwalls, rough and polished granite surfaces, and mirrored chrome—conceived by a Japanese firm with the arresting name Super Potato. At the center of it all, the glass-enclosed exhibition kitchen captures the limelight. Here, amid tanks of live lobsters and prawns, a versatile crew prepares their 21st-century version of four different types of cuisine: Italian, Asian, seafood and grilled dishes.

This innovative concept works well, allowing diners to take a culinary voyage from Asia (pad Thai and sushi) to Italy (papardelle Bolognese) and back to the U.S. (American Kobe-style beef tenderloin). Keeping pace with this world tour, the wine list spans the globe but its strength is Down Under (chef Martin Heierling hails from New Zealand).

You'll find Sensi past Bellagio's lobby, on the Via Fiore promenade.

Shibuya (MGM Grand)

064

Japanese ✗✗

3799 Las Vegas Blvd. S.

Phone:	702-891-3001	Dinner daily
Web:	www.mgmgrand.com	
Prices:	$$$	

MGM Mirage

From the room partitions fashioned of thin ribbons of wood to the backlit "canvas" of cube-shaped glass pieces that hangs above the sushi bar, Shibuya is as sleek and stylish as the Tokyo district for which the restaurant is named.

Expertise and an artful eye mark the preparation and presentation of the food here. Sushi lovers will appreciate the Shibuya roll (toasted nori and sticky rice wrapped around fresh snow-crab meat, red tuna, crunchy cucumber and creamy avocado), while the signature *toro* tartare with Beluga caviar and gold leaf appeals to high rollers. The chef's skill in balancing flavors best illustrates itself in the black cod marinated in nutty-sweet caramelized shiro miso and paired with a pungent, crispy shoot of ginger root.

If you're new to sake, ask the knowledgeable sake sommelier for help navigating the extensive list of rice wine.

Shintaro (Bellagio)

Japanese ✗✗

3600 Las Vegas Blvd. S.

Phone:	702-693-8255	Dinner daily
Web:	www.bellagio.com	
Prices:	$$$$	

The Strip

♿

MGM Mirage

A tiny Japanese garden announces Shintaro, located on the edge of Bellagio's casino floor. Inside, the first thing you see is the sushi bar, backed by multicolored backlit tanks, where live jellyfish float, ghostlike, in the water. Beyond the bar lies an elegant dining room accented by vibrant California colors and windows that look out on Lake Bellagio and its periodic fountain display. Traditional tables here share space with marble-topped *teppan yaki* tables, where chefs cook multicourse meals for eager groups.

Premium ingredients justify the high prices for superior sushi, a Pan-Asian tasting menu, and pleasing Pacific Rim preparations (think miso-glazed Chilean sea bass, pan-seared until it's crispy outside and tender inside). The wine list travels across the continents and ends up in Japan with a great selection of sake.

Smith & Wollensky

066

3767 Las Vegas Blvd. S. (bet Harmon & Tropicana Aves.)

Phone:	702-862-4100
Web:	www.smithandwollensky.com
Prices:	$$$$

Lunch & dinner daily

The Smith & Wollensky Restaurant Group

There's nothing small about this 635-seat steakhouse, brought to Vegas in 1998 as part of the well-known nationwide chain founded in Midtown Manhattan. USDA prime steaks (dry-aged and butchered in-house) weigh in at up to 18 ounces, and come with equally hefty price tags. As a starter, the shellfish "bouquet" overflows with lobster, oysters, shrimp, mussels, clams and "colossal" lump crabmeat. Sides, from French fries to truffled macaroni and cheese, are sized for two—no exceptions.

Freestanding in a green and white building across from the Monte Carlo, Smith & Wollensky opens its Grill for lunch and late-night dining seven days a week, and even offers sidewalk seats on The Strip. Those foolhardy enough to brave the perpetual evening gridlock on Las Vegas Boulevard can take advantage of the restaurant's valet parking (offered at dinner only).

91

Social House (Treasure Island)

Asian

3300 Las Vegas Blvd. S.

Phone:	702-894-7777	Dinner daily
Web:	www.socialhouselv.com	
Prices:	$$$	

MGM Mirage

Come graze with the glitterati at TI's new "it" restaurant. Take the elevator or climb the stairway lined with metal safe-deposit-like boxes to reach this oh-so-hip second-floor haunt. With its striking organic design by the New York firm AvroKo, Social House is the brainchild of the Pure Management Group (whose establishments include Pure and Tangerine).

The place is a bit schizophrenic, as if it can't decide between being a nightclub or a restaurant. And so it does both; DJs spin tunes each evening, and dining tables morph into conveyances for cocktails with the help of a hydraulic system. As expensive as it is expansive, the menu rolls out sushi and sashimi along with the likes of Kobe beef three ways, tamarind short ribs, and citrus peel miso-marinated cod.

Snag a seat on the outdoor patio for a front-row seat for the provocative Sirens of TI® show.

Spago (Caesars Palace)

068

The Forum Shops, 3500 Las Vegas Blvd. S.

Phone: 702-369-6300

Web: www.wolfgangpuck.com

Prices: **$$$**

Lunch & dinner daily

The Wolfgang Puck Fine Dining Group

The Strip

Beginning with the original Spago in Beverly Hills, Wolfgang Puck has taken his successful concept as far afield as Maui. Back in Vegas, this branch of Spago catches your eye as a casual Mediterranean cafe, one that blends right in on the main "street" of the Caesars Forum Shops.

The cafe sets a casual tone with its "outdoor" seating in the mall, around the corner from the Fountain of the Gods. Here, the menu is as relaxed as the ambience, offering a selection of pizzas, pastas, sandwiches and salads, along with a handful of moderately priced entrées. Inside, the sleek and airy dining room (open for dinner only) kicks the options up a notch with the likes of handmade chanterelle agnolotti, butter-poached Maine lobster, and Japanese Wagyu beef.

Just don't look for foie gras; as of spring 2007, Puck's restaurants no longer serve this politically incorrect delicacy.

STACK (Mirage)

069

3400 Las Vegas Blvd. S.

Phone: 702-791-7111   Dinner daily
Web: www.mirage.com
Prices: **$$$$**

The Strip

MGM Mirage

In 2006, the Mirage stacked the odds in its favor by polishing up its fading image with the opening of Love™, the Cirque de Soleil show set to The Beatle's music. And, of course, what's a little image-enhancing without a couple of trendy new restaurants?

STACK is one of these new additions. Layered with undulating wood strips suggesting the walls of Nevada's nearby Red Rock Canyon, the restaurant envelops diners under its dark ceiling amid flickering candlelight. In the front of the room, the cool curving bar is the place to people-watch while you sip on house libations like the S'mores STACK martini, made with Stoli Vanil, chocolate Godiva, and Starbucks coffee liqueur.

Ponder the menu before you decide on American fare like the shellfish STACK, mini Kobe chili-cheese dogs, or the bone-in Brooklyn filet with an "XL" twice-baked potato on the side.

Stripsteak (Mandalay Bay)

070

3950 Las Vegas Blvd. S.

Phone: 702-632-7414
Web: www.michaelmina.net
Prices: $$$$

Dinner daily

The Strip

MGM Mirage

Hungry guys that find themselves in Vegas wondering "Where's the beef?" will find it in spades at Michael Mina's first steakhouse concept. Long renowned for his skill preparing fish, Mina defies the beach theme at Mandalay Bay, delving instead into certified Angus beef. The result is one of the best steakhouses in Las Vegas, where the beef hangs to dry-age next to the exhibition kitchen.

A well-marbled, 10-ounce ribeye cap of Masami Farms American Kobe comes out moist, tender and buttery after being grilled over mesquite. If that's too small for you, try the 18-ounce bone-in ribeye, or the manly 30-ounce Porterhouse. Still hungry? Pair your steak with a butter-poached lobster tail or some grilled foie gras.

No matter your luck in the casino, go for broke here diet-wise and enjoy the trio of crisp and smoky duck-fat fries.

Sushi Roku (Caesars Palace)

Japanese ✗✗

071

The Forum Shops, 3500 Las Vegas Blvd. S.

Phone:	702-733-7373	Lunch & dinner daily
Web:	www.sushiroku.com	
Prices:	**$$**	

©Jeff Green/Innovative Dining

Sophisticated Sushi Roku seems right at home amid the statues, fountains and chi-chi shops on the third and top floor of the Forum Shops at Caesars Palace. Part of a small chain favored by the weight-conscious set in Los Angeles, where it was born, this little Japanese gem prides itself on the freshness and quality of its fish.

Exceptional Spanish mackerel, tender *toro* and sea urchin highlight the generous sushi menu, while preparations such as whole crispy sea bass "Shanghai style," and rock-shrimp tempura with jalapeño add international spark. For fashionistas, a meal of low-calorie sushi will leave you none the heavier to fit into that designer dress you've been eyeing in the mall.

Dark woods, bamboo, stone, and cascading water create a Zen vibe that is at once both cozy and contemporary. Service is prompt and stylish.

SW Steakhouse (Wynn)

Steakhouse XXX

072

3131 Las Vegas Blvd. S.

Phone:	702-770-3325	Dinner daily
Web:	www.wynnlasvegas.com	
Prices:	**$$$$**	

Wynn Las Vegas

Descend the spiral escalator from the casino level under a canopy of colorful parasols and you'll find Steve Wynn's idea of a steakhouse. Sleek and polished, the dining room affords dramatic views of the hotel's water feature, Lake of Dreams. A seat on the spacious outdoor terrace gets you even closer, and the streaming water wall provides a serene backdrop. Service is as polished as the décor, with personable waiters seeing to a casual-chic clientele.

An ambitious kitchen team pushes the cuisine a cut above your usual steaks and chops. Sure, there are prime steaks aplenty, but cedar-roasted Kumamoto oysters topped with crispy pancetta and roasted leeks, and olive-oil-poached Scottish salmon will give you an inkling of the menu's versatility. Desserts (angel food cake with strawberry compote, Meyer lemon ice cream and strawberry sorbet) are as strong as the savory courses.

Tableau (Wynn)

American 🍴🍴🍴

The Strip

3131 Las Vegas Blvd. S.

Phone: 702-248-3463   Lunch & dinner daily
Web: www.wynnlasvegas.com
Prices: **$$$$**

Wynn Las Vegas

Tableau is an apt description of Wynn's signature restaurant, set off the separate lobby for the hotel's exclusive Tower Suites. And a lovely picture it is: imagine a luminous scene in which embroidered ecru draperies soften the windows, deep crown moldings line the ceiling, and crystal chandeliers cast a sparkling glow over the room's cream and salmon-pink palette. In the adjoining rotunda-like space, windows frame the pool and cabanas of the Fairway Villas.

It is in this elegant *atelier* that chef Mark LoRusso painstakingly paints his own picture of American fare, using a classic approach while respecting the integrity of the best ingredients. A plump square of Dungeness crab, deep-fried and served with clam-chowder "sauce," or a pear- and blue-cheese-stuffed veal chop shine as à la carte *chef-d'œuvres*, while two nightly tasting menus add to the gallery of fine cuisine.

Tao (Venetian)

074

3355 Las Vegas Blvd. S.

Phone:	702-388-8338	Dinner daily
Web:	www.taolasvegas.com	
Prices:	**$$$**	

The Strip

The Venetian

Larger than life is one way to describe this three-level, 42,000-square-foot restaurant and nightclub that made its splashy debut on the Vegas scene in 2005. No expense was seemingly spared in the design: gray stone water-filled vessels afloat with rose petals and flickering candles line the entrance; a 20-foot-tall statue of Buddha presides over a shimmering pool in the main dining room; and a collection of hand-carved opium pipes fills one accent wall.

Once you get over the opulent décor, set your sights on the Asian menu. Premium ingredients and skillful preparation ensure that the sushi is just-off-the-boat fresh, the crispy spring rolls are plump with roasted Peking duck, and the miso-glazed Chilean sea bass is moist and fork-tender.

Go to eat, and stay to party; the third level rocks at night as one of the hottest clubs on The Strip.

Taqueria Cañonita (Venetian)

075

Grand Canal Shoppes, 3377 Las Vegas Blvd. S.

Phone:	702-414-3773	Lunch & dinner daily
Web:	www.venetian.com	
Prices:	$$$$	

The Strip

E Brands Restaurants

Only in Vegas can you dine on "Mexico City soul food" on the banks of a Venetian canal, complete with gondoliers belting out Italian arias in the background. If this sounds like fun to you, make your way to Taqueria Cañonita, located in the Grand Canal Shoppes at The Venetian. The restaurant's stone terrace rims the canal, giving the illusion of outdoor dining under a realistic-looking painted sky.

Hearty portions of Mexican favorites (flavorful *carne asada Norteña*) are crafted using traditional spices and high-quality products, such as the fresh corn tortillas handmade in house. For dessert, indulge in the *bunuelos con canela*, the Mexican version of a Napoleon. Crunchy squares of fried dough are layered with nutty mascarpone cream and cinnamon-spiced roasted peaches, and crowned with vanilla-bean ice cream—a sweet ending indeed.

Top of the World (Stratosphere)

American ✗✗

076

2000 Las Vegas Blvd. S.

Phone:	702-380-7711	Lunch & dinner daily
Web:	www.topoftheworldlv.com	
Prices:	$$$	

&

©Bob Burchess

Acrophobics need not apply at this lofty restaurant, which looms 832 feet in the air at the top of the Stratosphere Tower. But if you crave an unparalleled 360-degree view of The Strip in all its glittering glory, you've come to the right place.

You won't find a better vista than at this special-occasion space, where the multicourse menus for two nourish celebrations with the likes of chateaubriand and the signature chocolate Stratosphere for dessert. Don't expect the level of food to match the height of the tower, though; this is a place where view definitely trumps cuisine.

Because Top of the World is so popular with visitors, reservations are recommended for lunch, and required for dinner. A full revolution takes about an hour and twenty minutes to complete, so you won't miss an angle during your meal. All you have to do it sit there ... and rotate.

Trattoria del Lupo (Mandalay Bay)

Italian ✗✗

077

3950 Las Vegas Blvd. S.

Phone:	702-740-5522	Dinner daily
Web:	www.wolfgangpuck.com	
Prices:	$$$	

MGM Mirage

Wolfgang Puck's casual cafe, set on a stone-lined restaurant row just off the casino floor, evokes an Italian trattoria with its closely clustered tables, pastel colors, antique furnishings, large central bar and airy indoor patio.

Exhibition pizza, antipasto and dessert stations give diners a look at the careful technique that marks each straightforward dish here. Bold flavors harmonize equally well in a simple starter of shaved Italian meats, arranged around a ramekin of spicy oil-cured olives, peppers and dried cranberries, or a signature pizza topped with tiger shrimp, braised pancetta and leeks. Pastas are made fresh on the premises.

For dessert, a warm panini made of sweet Italian egg bread scented with honey and vanilla and enclosing a filling of creamy, rich hazelnut butter will make you howl with pleasure.

Trevi (Caesars Palace)

Italian XX

078

The Forum Shops, 3500 Las Vegas Blvd. S.

Phone:	702-735-4663	Lunch & dinner daily
Web:	www.trevi-italian.com	
Prices:	$$	

The Strip

Trevi

With a name like Trevi, what better location could this trattoria have than hard by the Baroque Fountain of the Gods in the Caesars Forum Shops? Trevi's mall terrace with its walk-up gelato/espresso bar abuts the fountain, while inside, a 12-foot-high orange chandelier made of blown glass forms the centerpiece of the circular, bi-level dining room (which, until early 2007, housed Bertolini's restaurant).

A meal here begins with a loaf of warm bread wrapped in an Italian newspaper (okay, it's fake, but who cares?), and maybe an Italian margarita, spiked with Grand Marnier and Amaretto. Then it's on to brick-oven-fired pizzas, specialty pastas, or entrées such as veal piccata and chicken Marsala. And, though the food may not be absolutely authentic, the setting is the best thing this side of Rome—before you leave, throw a coin in the fountain and make a wish to return.

Valentino (Venetian)

Italian XXX

079

3355 Las Vegas Blvd. S.

Phone:	702-414-3000	Lunch & dinner daily
Web:	www.valentinolv.com	
Prices:	$$$$	

The Strip

The Venetian

Sister to Valentino in Los Angeles, the Santa Monica stalwart of Sicilian-born restaurateur Piero Selvaggio for more than 30 years, this version debuted on the Vegas Strip in 1998. Inside, the boisterous and casual grill gives way to the more refined dining rooms beyond, which received a recent redesign in tones of teal with copper accents.

Executive chef/partner Luciano Pellegrini commands the kitchen, improvising his creative takes on pasta and gnocchi as well as roasted branzino, and Kobe-style beef braised in Barolo. If you don't see anything to suit your fancy on the regular menu, Valentino will accommodate by allowing you to order dishes off the tasting menus as à la carte items—a rare offer, indeed.

High rollers with their entourage in tow have an option of several private dining spaces, including the intimate Barolo Room, a private wine cellar that seats only four.

Verandah (Four Seasons)

American ✕✕✕

080

3960 Las Vegas Blvd. S.

Phone: 702-632-5121   Lunch & dinner daily
Web: www.fourseasons.com/lasvegas
Prices: $$$

©Larry Hanna/Verandah

With the air of a gracious southern porch, Verandah conjures up visions of sipping mint juleps amid leafy palms overlooking lush landscaping and the Four Seasons' pool. Soft greens and warm woods foster the natural feel, while an L-shaped outdoor terrace—a popular spot for a tranquil repast—doubles the dining space.

This casual setting marries well with simple dishes made from flavorful products. Meal options include breakfast, lunch, dinner and an oh-so-civilized afternoon tea (served Monday through Thursday). At dinner, Italian influences color menu selections such as chicken scallopine, *branzino al forno*, and spaghetti *alla carbonara*. Or have it your way, and order your choice of entrée, starch, vegetable and sauce.

The restaurant's location just past the hotel's conference rooms assures that Verandah attracts a solid stream of business people, especially at lunch.

Wing Lei ✿ (Wynn)

Chinese XXXX

081

3131 Las Vegas Blvd. S.

Phone:	702-248-3463	Dinner daily
Web:	www.wynnlasvegas.com	
Prices:	$$$$	

Wynn Las Vegas

In keeping with the sumptuous tone of the Wynn resort, Wing Lei dresses in Imperial splendor. Abalone, mother-of-pearl and 14-carat gold accent the opulent room, while windows peer out on a black marble Botero sculpture flanked by 100-year-old pomegranate trees.

A native of Taiwan, chef Richard Chen entices diners with his haute Chinese cuisine. Using a "reverse fusion" technique, the chef evokes the seasons with a beautifully balanced composed salad of peekytoe crab, diced avocado, and sweet mango; or fragrant basil chicken in a clay pot, made with organic birds from Sonoma, California. The multicourse Peking duck menu magnifies this product in several different preparations, making a meal fit for an emperor.

The name? It derives from the Chinese character created for the Wynn resort; not surprisingly, that character translates in English as "forever prosperous."

Appetizers

- Peking Duck Salad with Almond, Orange, Truffle Vinaigrette
- Peekytoe Crab Salad with Avocado, Mango, Citrus Dressing
- Marinated Black Cod with Crispy Noodle

Entrées

- Chilean Sea Bass, Baby Bok Choy, Soya Ginger Sherry Broth
- Garlic Beef Tenderloin, Garlic Chips, Choy Sum
- Sesame-crusted Halibut, Scallion Radish Salad, Soy Orange Glaze

Desserts

- Strawberry Tart, Chantilly, Strawberry Cheesecake Ice Cream
- Milk Chocolate Brûlée Bar, Caramel Cream, Hazelnut Crust
- Lemon Sorbet Gâteau, Lemon Cream, Nougatine

FINE DINING WATER FROM TUSCANY

East of The Strip

EAST OF THE STRIP

It's business, brains and basketball east of The Strip, with the commercial district, Las Vegas Convention Center, McCarran International Airport and the University of Nevada at Las Vegas (UNLV). Some newer casinos and non-gaming hotels are located here as well, but many locals favor the smaller, less glitzy places on the old Boulder Strip. To abandon the neon altogether head for **Lake Mead**, the largest man-made lake in the U.S. Its National Recreation Area offers 1-1/2-million acres of outdoor fun.

CASINOS AND ANCIENT CULTURES

Between The Strip and Lake Mead, **Henderson** is Nevada's second-largest and America's fastest-growing city. Once a working-class factory town in the desert, it's now a place of placid waters and pastoral pleasures attracting the affluent to its planned communities. Green Valley was the first, and set the pace with its verdant landscaping and serious golf and shopping. Family-friendliness and wholesome recreation aside, this is still Vegas. Green Valley is

Las Vegas News Bureau

home to one of the area's luxury casino resorts, Green Valley Ranch. On nearby **Lake Las Vegas** you'll find other opulent casinos and lodgings, along with world-class golf courses, fine dining, and high-end shopping in a setting more like Tuscany than the desert.

Twenty miles farther to the southeast is Sin City's polar opposite. **Boulder City** was built in 1929 to accommodate **Hoover Dam** workers and their families. There's plenty of charm but not a slot machine to be had in Nevada's only gambling-free

town. The engineering marvel that Boulder City's citizens built down the road, however, spurred Las Vegas's gaming industry after the railroad left Vegas behind.

A visit to Overton, on Lake Mead's north end, will remind you that, long before neon, nature and native cultures performed dazzling feats here. The **Lost City Museum** houses artifacts of people who dwelled in the cliffs 1,000 years ago. Admire their petroglyphs and the red sandstone formations created by wind and water during the Jurassic Period at **Valley of Fire State Park.**

A.J.'s Steakhouse (Hard Rock)

082

Steakhouse ✕✕✕

4455 Paradise Rd.

Phone: 702-693-5500
Web: www.hardrockhotel.com
Prices: $$$

Tue – Sat dinner only

A.J.'s Steakhouse

When you walk through the leather door at A.J.'s in the Hard Rock Hotel *(see hotel listing)*, you'll be transported back to the early days of Vegas, when several rounds of drinks topped off by a cigarette was considered a good meal. Rest assured that the bar here pours plenty of martinis, but now it's in a smoke-free environment.

Settle back into the swanky space and wax nostalgic as the piano man plays homage to Rat Pack crooners. As you peruse the menu, the aromas of grilled meat will waft through the room from the open kitchen, making your meal decisions more difficult. Should you start with the house crab cakes, the garlicky shrimp scampi, or a crisp wedge of iceberg napped with blue cheese? If you're really hungry, go for the manly main course: a 20-ounce prime New York sirloin.

Note that dishes are priced à la carte, so the bill could be as hefty as your steak.

Bistro Zinc (MonteLago Village)

083

15 Via Bel Canto, Henderson

Phone: 702-567-9462
Web: www.bistrozincrestaurant.com
Prices: $$

Tue – Sun lunch & dinner
Mon dinner only

MonteLago Village Resort

Tuscan villa outside, French bistro inside, American approach throughout—Joseph Keller's (yes, that Keller) Bistro Zinc in MonteLago Village is hard to pin down. Its décor hints of brother Thomas' Bouchon in Napa Valley (think zinc counter, raw bar, specials chalked on a blackboard), but like the sports on its big-screen TV and the rock music on the stereo, Zinc's cuisine plays out American.

Cajun fare shows up at lunch with po' boy sandwiches, and again at dinner with seafood gumbo. A house specialty, chicken potpie shares menu space with a classic French Muscovy duck breast and leg confit. Tartare speaks French and Californian—Kobe beef with Dijon, olive oil and quail egg, or yellowfin tuna with avocado and pickled cucumber.

There's live jazz outside some evenings, a jazz brunch on Sundays, and a jazzy riff on tried-and-true cuisine—wherever it comes from—all the time.

Como's (MonteLago Village)

084

American 🍴

10 Via Brianza, Henderson

Phone:	702-567-9950	Lunch & dinner daily
Web:	www.comosllv.com	
Prices:	$$$	

MonteLago Village Resort

The Strip isn't the only place in Vegas enjoying gourmet enlightenment. This comfy-chic spot in MonteLago Village shines as a fine-dining alternative at Lake Las Vegas.

While the restaurant's name suggests the famous lake in northern Italy, the cuisine holds to this side of the Atlantic. Beef—braised, slow-roasted, grilled—steals the leading role at dinner, with optional accompaniments like lobster tail, foie gras truffle butter or "Oscar" (crab, asparagus and béarnaise) to gild the lily. Fish, poultry, pork and lamb satisfy those wanting "anything but beef." Como's kitchen kicks up the standard iceberg-lettuce wedge with heirloom tomatoes, and a lovely tuna tartare with avocado, tapenade, basil and aged balsamic illustrates the tasteful tweaking you'll find here.

There are interesting twists at the cocktail bar too. Who says the classics have to be boring?

Firefly

085

3900 Paradise Rd. (bet. Corporate Dr. & E. Twain Ave.)

Lunch & dinner daily

Phone: 702-369-3971
Web: www.fireflylv.com
Prices: ☕

East of The Strip

©Mark Gibson

For a late-night nosh, twenty-somethings flit to this tapas bar on busy Paradise Road just east of The Strip. Firefly is open until 3am on Friday and Saturday, and until 2am every other night, but you don't have to be a hard-core partier to enjoy the family-style small plates in this lively, club-like restaurant.

Since the minimalist-chic décor didn't cost millions of dollars, the prices here are affordable, especially compared to nearby resorts on The Strip. So round up your own bunch of revelers, get into the beat of the Latin music, and order up a pitcher of refreshing sangria to go with the parade of hot and cold tapas. Whether you dip your mini grilled brie sandwich into a bowl of tasty tomato soup, share a plate of panko-crusted fish sticks, or dive into a flaky mushroom tart, this Firefly is the bug to catch.

Gandhi

East of The Strip

4080 Paradise Rd. (at Flamingo Rd.)

Phone: 702-734-0094
Web: www.gandhicuisine.com
Prices: 🍪🍪

Lunch & dinner daily

©Mark Gibson

Locals know to seek out Gandhi, tucked behind Morton's Steakhouse in an unassuming little strip mall, for an epicurean tour through Kolkata, Bangalore and Mumbai. At lunch, choices are limited to the buffet, but who's complaining? An extremely affordable and bounteous array of Northern and Southern Indian dishes are labeled with a short description for newcomers to this type of cuisine. So go ahead and sample—the buffet is a great opportunity to be adventurous and taste some new things. Dinner brings a full menu of tandoori specialties, tempting rice dishes, seafood delicacies and curries, including many vegetarian options.

The large, airy room with its soaring ceilings and lofty mezzanine seating belies the restaurant's modest façade. Suspended just below the ceiling, an enormous tapestry buffers noise while blanketing the room in primary colors.

Hank's Fine Steaks & Martinis
(Green Valley Ranch)

Steakhouse ✗✗✗

2300 Paseo Verde Pkwy., Henderson

Dinner daily

Phone: 702-617-7515
Web: www.greenvalleyranchresort.com
Prices: $$$$

Station Casinos

Journalist, Green Valley developer, and all-around local icon Hank Greenspun (1909-89) had a big hand in shaping Las Vegas, so a place named for him had better be up to snuff. Hank would likely approve of the flagship restaurant at Green Valley Ranch Resort *(see hotel listing)*. The opulent interior with crystal chandeliers glistening over dark wood, leather-upholstered chairs and gray-blue booths recalls Hank's early days in classy, late-1940s Vegas in an updated way. So does the food. Pricey but good, prime dry-aged beef is the focus of the menu. Among the sides, the truffled tater tots (tiny crisp-tender potato croquettes drizzled with truffle oil and dusted with parmesan) make a tasty accompaniment to the beef.

Stop first in the piano lounge—you haven't been here until you've sampled at least one of the 30 martinis from the glamorous backlit onyx bar.

Hofbräuhaus

088

4510 Paradise Rd. (at Harmon Ave.)

Phone:	702-853-2337	Lunch & dinner daily
Web:	www.hofbrauhauslasvegas.com	
Prices:		

Hofbräuhaus

If you missed Oktoberfest, head to Hofbräuhaus for an authentic German beer-hall experience. A perfect reproduction of Hofbräuhaus München, commissioned by Duke Wilhelm V in 1589, this lively restaurant boasts hand-painted cathedral ceilings and seating for some 800 diners, between the *Schwemme* (beer hall) and the temperature-controlled *biergarten*.

Strangers come together here at long, wooden, communal tables to down liters of *weissbier* and *dunkel brau* and dig into Bavarian specialties such as *sauerbraten, Jägerschnitzel*, and the house *wurstplatte*. After a couple of beers, you'll be singing along with the German band that entertains diners nightly. Just when you're convinced you're in Munich, though, the band breaks into "Viva Las Vegas."

Bring the whole family; there's a short children's menu, and even a magician to delight the kids.

India Palace

089

505 E. Twain Ave. (bet. Paradise Rd. & Swenson St.)

Lunch & dinner daily

Phone: 702-796-4177
Web: N/A
Prices: 🍜

©Mark Gibson

A feast for the eyes as well as the stomach awaits you at the lunch buffet at India Palace. Served seven days a week, this extravaganza lays out a colorful array of North and South Indian fare. Dishes like vegetable *pakora*, chicken *biryani*, *sag paneer*, and *dal makhani* boast pronounced flavors elevated by exotic spices. For novices, the buffet offerings are labeled to dispel any mystery, but half the fun is trying new things and all of them are good. Best of all, can eat as much as you want for just under $10—that's a bargain any way you slice it. If you can't make it for lunch, dinner prices are moderate, service is friendly and prompt, and you're bound to find something you like on the expansive menu.

Never mind about the bland storefront façade—your mother was right when she told you not to judge a book by its cover.

Lindo Michoacán

Mexican ✗

2655 E. Desert Inn Rd. (bet. McLeod Dr. & S. Eastern Ave.)

Phone:	702-735-6828	Lunch & dinner daily
Web:	www.lindomichoacancatering.com	
Prices:	$$	

©Mark Gibson

You'll have to leave The Strip behind to savor the authentic cuisine of the Michoacán region of Mexico in Las Vegas. At Lindo, chef/owner Javier Barajas raises the stakes on Mexican food with his adventurous menu.

Sure, you can be safe and order standards like burritos, tacos and fajitas, but why not go for broke—you're in Vegas, after all—and try something different? You'll find the likes of *nopalitos* (Mexican cactus) grilled with onions, tomatoes, cilantro and jalapeños, and *birria de chivo* (a Mexican festival dish made with goat meat cooked in beer with dried chiles and spices) *muy delicioso*. And since Barajas' doctor put him on a heart-healthy diet, he has dumped the traditional lard in favor of vegetable and olive oils in his dishes.

Special lunch combinations (served from 11am to 5pm) are a bargain at under $11.

Lotus of Siam

091

Thai ✗

953 E. Sahara Ave. (bet. Maryland Pkwy & Paradise Rd.)

Phone:	702-735-3033	Mon – Fri lunch & dinner
Web:	www.saipinchutima.com	Sat – Sun dinner only
Prices:	$$	

Jakrapan Atcharawan

This hole-in-the-wall Thai restaurant brightens up the down-in-the-mouth Sahara Commercial Center with its vibrant flavors and spices. What the plain dining room lacks in ambience it more than makes up for in its cuisine, and locals and visitors in the know have uncovered the secret of tasty Thai dishes here.

A virtual encyclopedia of Thai favorites fills the regular menu, while the separate Northern menu highlights the milder specialties of this region of Thailand, sparked by influences from Laos, Myanmar, and the Hunan area of South China. Marinated prawns wrapped with bacon in a rice-paper crêpe, roast-duck curry, and deep-fried whole catfish topped with chiles, garlic and Thai basil will transport your taste buds to another continent, while the wine list is heavy with German varietals that pair well with spicy food.

Lucille's Smokehouse Barbeque

Barbecue 🍴

East of The Strip

2245 Village Walk Dr. (at Paseo Verde Pkwy.), Henderson

Phone: 702-257-7427   Lunch & dinner daily
Web: www.lucillesbbq.com
Prices: **$$**

©Mark Gibson

If sitting on the porch at this California-based barbecue chain and watching the ceiling fans whirl to rhythm-and-blues tunes doesn't put you in a down-home state of mind, the food surely will.

Located in The District shopping center near Green Valley Ranch Resort *(see hotel listing)*, Lucille Buchanan's Vegas outpost features Tex-Mex and Cajun specials, but country cooking and barbecue star. Start off with a taste of Southern-fried: green tomatoes, okra, dill pickles. Then tuck into some serious barbecue, which covers the range of chicken, pork and beef, all slow-smoked over hickory and served with homemade biscuits and smoky-sweet house sauce.

Silverware is provided, but this food begs to be eaten with your fingers, making Lucille's a good choice for families or groups that don't mind messy hands (warm moist towels are presented when you're done).

Luna Rossa (MonteLago Village)

Italian ✗✗

10 Via Bel Canto, Henderson

Phone: 702-568-9921
Web: N/A
Prices: $$

Lunch & dinner daily

East of The Strip

MonteLago Village Resort

Sitting on the patio overlooking Lake Las Vegas, you could easily believe you're in Luna Rossa, the town on the Adriatic with which this stylish Italian establishment—the only serious Italian restaurant in MonteLago Village—shares its name. Inside, you'll also find a charming space, understatedly elegant with blond wood and white upholstery.

Insalata caprese, creamy penne *alla vodka*, veal scallopini, and comforting *pollo alla pizzaiola* (chicken with mozzarella, spinach and tomato sauce) will be familiar friends to cognoscenti of traditional *cucina italiana*. In the risotto *ai frutti del mare* you may even taste the Adriatic coast.

Wine is taken as seriously here as the food; the knowledgeable staff can suggest an appropriate glass or two. But if you forget where you are, don't blame the *vino*. You've just been enchanted by *la luna rossa* ("the red moon").

123

Marrakech

3900 Paradise Rd. (at Corporate Dr.)

Phone:	702-737-5611	Dinner daily
Web:	N/A	
Prices:	$$	

East of The Strip

©Mark Gibson

A different kind of desert oasis, Marrakech introduced Las Vegas diners to Moroccan food in 1979. Family-style meals still pack in crowds around the lovely inlaid-wood tables, where they feast on a traditional, six-course prix-fixe repast beginning with the likes of Moroccan-style shrimp scampi and ending with a sweet take on classic *b'stilla* (a phyllo-dough pastry stuffed with nuts, fruit and sugar, then sprinkled with powdered sugar and cinnamon). The main attraction is the couscous platter, crowned with a Cornish game hen (a vegetarian version is also available).

Tent-like fabric billows from the dining-room ceiling as colored-glass lanterns cast a dusky glow over luxurious tapestries, copper urns and blue-tiled archways. In the evening, belly dancers encourage customer participation as they shimmy to the upbeat North African music.

Marssa (Loews)

Asian XX

101 Montelago Blvd., Henderson

Phone: 702-567-6000
Web: www.loewshotels.com
Prices: $$$

Mon – Sat dinner only

East of The Strip

Loews Hotels

An Asian oasis in the midst of an otherwise Moroccan-inspired atmosphere, Marssa is the fine-dining option at the Loews Lake Las Vegas Resort *(see hotel listing).* (It was formerly called Japengo when the hotel was a Hyatt.) *Marssa* means "by the sea," in this case the Pacific Rim, which inspires an exciting menu that emphasizes, but is not limited to, seafood.

Szechwan pepper beef noodles in garlic chile broth sounds intriguing, but the serious sushi is hard to pass up. *Opakapaka lau lau,* Hawaiian snapper wrapped in banana leaves with coconut ginger sauce, kabocha squash and banana chutney exemplifies the exotic offerings that show a deft and delectable balance of assertive flavors.

Refined service and elegant touches such as orchids, candlelight and Asian-inspired china complement the artfully presented cuisine, as do the comprehensive wine and sake lists.

Medici Café
(Ritz-Carlton Lake Las Vegas)

Contemporary ✗✗✗

1610 Lake Las Vegas Pkwy., Henderson

Phone: 702-567-4700
Web: www.ritz-carlton.com
Prices: **$$$**

Lunch & dinner daily

The Ritz-Carlton

Housed in the Ritz-Carlton Lake Las Vegas *(see hotel listing)*, Medici Café visually lives up to its noble Tuscan name. The lovely terrace looks onto the hotel's Florentine garden, while Italianate furnishings and reproductions of Renaissance art grace the interior. More a princely dining retreat than a formal hall, the space is just right for another kind of renaissance, which is reflected in the display kitchen and its ambitious contemporary menu.

Reviving classic American fare like pan-roasted chicken doesn't prevent the kitchen from venturing abroad, however, especially back to the Mediterranean. Pan-roasted halibut is accented with saffron, basil and preserved lemon—flavors the Medici would have enjoyed. And they surely would have saved room for the signature chocolate soufflé.

Changing with the seasons, the chef's tasting menu comes with optional wine pairings.

MiraLago

Contemporary ✕✕

75 Montelago Blvd., Henderson

Phone: 702-568-7383
Web: www.lakelasvegas.com
Prices: $$

Tue – Sat lunch & dinner
Sun – Mon lunch only

East of The Strip

Lake Las Vegas Resort

Located in the Reflection Bay Golf Club at Lake Las Vegas Resort, this cafe is a refreshing spot for lunch, dinner or Sunday brunch. Thanks to the courteous staff, you'll feel like a member the moment you enter.

Though tables in the dining room enjoy views of the desert hills and the lake, the terrace is the place to be. A table here, under the shade of cheerful umbrellas and swaying palms, brings you even closer to the water.

Mediterranean accents begin the dinner menu with sautéed calamari paired with Roma tomatoes, proscuitto, olives, capers and a white-wine butter sauce. Entrées range from pan-seared Nantucket sea scallops with lobster pancetta mashed potatoes to herbed rack of lamb in a pomegranate reduction. At lunch, signature sandwiches (a lobster club wrap with gouda and pancetta) vie with the specialties (chicken cavatappi in garlic cream) for attention.

Nobu ✿ (Hard Rock)

098

4455 Paradise Rd.

Phone: 702-693-5090   Dinner daily
Web: www.hardrockhotel.com
Prices: $$$$

East of The Strip

Hard Rock Hotel

Chef Nobu Matsuhisa burst on the New York City dining scene in 1994, when he opened his eponymous restaurant with partners Drew Nieporent and Robert DeNiro. Since then, the award-winning chef has expanded to locations across the globe. In Las Vegas, Nobu has hit the jackpot in its home at the Hard Rock Hotel *(see hotel listing)*.

Polished river rock forms the backdrop for the sushi bar, where chefs with hands more deft than those of the dealers in the casino prepare the freshest fish flown in from the market in Tokyo. Seductive sushi and sashimi (thinly sliced yellowtail served with small rings of Serrano chile; delicate Japanese snapper topped with crumbles of dry miso) are the hands-down winners here, but cash in on Nobu's miso-marinated black cod for a wonderful dish.

A wide range of sake complements the short but intelligently selected wine list.

Appetizers	*Entrées*	*Desserts*
• Yellowtail Sashimi with Jalapeño	• Black Cod with Miso	• Bento Box
• Mixed Seafood Ceviche	• Chilean Sea Bass with Black Bean Sauce or Dried Miso	• Hibiscus Champagne Cocktail
• Spicy Miso "Chips" with Tuna or Scallops	• Rock Shrimp Tempura with Butter Ponzu or Creamy Spicy Sauce	• Chestnut, Chocolate and Pears

LOUIS ROEDERER

CHAMPAGNE

Origin India

099

Indian ✗✗

4480 Paradise Rd. (at Harmon Rd.)

Phone: 702-734-6342
Web: www.originindiarestaurant.com
Prices: **$$**

Lunch & dinner daily

Origin India

Looking at the darkly tinted windows on the façade of Origin India, you'd never guess that a chic, contemporary décor dresses up the dining space inside. Located in a newer strip mall facing the Hard Rock Hotel, this inviting neighborhood restaurant dishes up bold, fresh flavors in every bite.

At lunch, specialties such as lamb *nihari* (slow-cooked and mildly spiced) or *chana masala* (buttery chickpeas stewed with onion, garlic, ginger and other pungent Indian spices) are a great deal, with reasonable prices and copious quantities of delicious food. Come dinnertime, tandoori dishes and other entrées are available in both meat and vegetarian versions.

Blond wood floors, high-backed dark leather chairs and wrought-iron light fixtures add to the pleasant ambience fostered by polite, attentive servers. Curtained alcoves provide niches for private dining.

Pasta Shop & Ristorante

East of The Strip

2495 E. Tropicana Ave. (bet. S. Eastern Ave. & Topaz St.)

Phone: 702-451-1893   Dinner daily
Web: www.pastashop.com
Prices: $$

Pasta Shop Ristorante

Old World charm meets nouveau chic in this eclectic yellow room, decorated by paintings for sale and square tables set with zebra-striped tablecloths and red napkins.

Brothers David and Glenn Alenik (originally from upstate New York) are justifiably renowned locally for their handmade pastas. Linguini with clams; lasagna made with four types of cheese, basil pesto and sweet Italian sausage; and squid-ink fettucini in a sweet saffron cream sauce topped by sautéed shrimp are just a few of the dishes that will make you glad you tore yourself away from The Strip. And to top it off, prices are moderate and all entrées come with a Caesar salad and garlic bread.

The restaurant even offers fresh pasta by the pound (this venture began as a wholesale pasta business) for those who want to take some home and steal all the credit.

Piero's

Italian ✗✗✗

101

355 Convention Center Dr. (at Paradise Rd.)

Phone: 702-369-2305   Dinner daily
Web: www.pieroscuisine.com
Prices: $$$

East of The Strip

Piero's

Founded by Freddie Glusman in 1982, this old-style Vegas restaurant has been in its present location across from the Las Vegas Convention Center since 1986. Here, it lures a steady stream of conventioneers and notables (a list of celebrity patrons is posted, if you're interested) who come for the likes of crispy fried calamari, tender osso buco, and spinach-stuffed *agnollotti alla crema* delivered by white-tuxedo-clad waiters.

Piero's, with its Aldo Luongo lithographs, original oil paintings and tiger-striped carpeting, stood in for one of the Mob hangouts in Martin Scorsese's 1995 film *Casino*. Despite the restaurant's generous size (nine separate dining rooms can seat 345 diners), it's best to make reservations as the place fills up quickly. If you do decide to drop in on a busy night, try for first-come, first-served seating at one of the black-granite bars.

Pink Taco (Hard Rock)

Mexican ✂

4455 Paradise Rd.

Phone: 702-693-5000
Web: www.hardrockhotel.com
Prices: $$

Lunch & dinner daily

Hard Rock Hotel

East of The Strip

Every day's a party at the Pink Taco, which fits right in at the Hard Rock Hotel *(see hotel listing)* with its pulsing music and vibrant décor enhanced by Mexican folk art. The later it gets, the more this place rocks.

A meal here starts, of course, with a complimentary bowl of freshly fried tortilla chips and a trio of salsas. Then, perhaps, the signature *panucho* (pink taco), a corn tortilla stuffed with beans and topped with grilled chicken, salsa roja, pickled onions and avocado ... or maybe a traditional burrito, or baby back ribs marinated in watermelon barbecue sauce and brushed with a tamarind glaze.

The large bar showcases an extensive selection of tequilas, margaritas and *cervezas*. Drop by Monday through Friday for happy hour (4pm to 7pm), when you can slam down two-for-one beers and house margaritas along with half-price appetizers.

The Restaurant at Platinum

Contemporary XXX

103

211 E. Flamingo Rd. (at Koval Ln.)

Phone:	702-636-2525	Lunch & dinner daily
Web:	www.theplatinumhotel.com	
Prices:	$$$	

Platinum

The new non-gaming, non-smoking, all-suites Platinum Hotel *(see hotel listing)* is home to this urbane and romantic dining room, done in a palette of cool blue and chocolate brown. On the fifth floor, Platinum the restaurant overlooks the hotel pool through a wall of glass, with The Strip glimmering in the distance.

If a menu is going to take risks, a city whose bread and butter is gambling is surely the place to do it. Even so, ambitious combinations and innovative techniques yield varied results here. Noodles made from extruded prawn meat in a salmon Pad Thai starter, for example, are no match for the sublime flavor and texture of the red wine and truffle-"draped" beef tenderloin.

The silver lining? Many items on the dinner menu are available as full-sized entrées or as "micro-plates," giving diners the flexibility to experience a wider array of dishes.

Simon Kitchen & Bar (Hard Rock)

Fusion XX

4455 Paradise Rd.

Phone: 702-693-4440
Web: www.hardrockhotel.com
Prices: $$$

Dinner daily

Bill Milne/Hard Rock Hotel

Between his rock-star good looks, charming personality and talent in the kitchen, chef Kerry Simon is a natural fit for the Hard Rock Hotel *(see hotel listing)*. In 2004 Simon and restaurateur Elizabeth Blau (who developed restaurants in Wynn and Bellagio) joined forces to open this Vegas hotspot, where the scene rocks with loud music and hip décor.

The chef doesn't limit himself to one type of cuisine. Instead, the menu bounces from tuna tataki lettuce wraps to wood-roasted pizzas to bamboo-steamed fish to filet mignon to spaghetti and meatballs. And it's all good.

For dessert, indulge your inner child and order Simon's Junk Food Sampler, an assortment of childhood favorites—the chef's riff on Rice Krispies Treats®, Hostess cream-filled cupcakes, pink "snowballs," and a chocolate milkshake—all grown up. Or go for the ultimate retro treat: a poof of pink cotton candy.

East of The Strip

Todd's Unique Dining

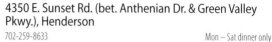
Fusion ✗

4350 E. Sunset Rd. (bet. Anthenian Dr. & Green Valley Pkwy.), Henderson

Phone: 702-259-8633
Web: www.toddsunique.com
Prices: $$$

Mon – Sat dinner only

East of The Strip

©Mark Gibson

Chef Todd Clore left the glamour of The Strip for this humble strip-mall location where locals hang at the bar, and those wanting something cozier take the booths on the opposite side.

Not wanting to tie himself down to any specific cuisine type, the chef bills his food as "unique," combining this, that, and whatever is fresh at the market each day. The menu veers toward Asia in the crispy curried chicken and pea-sprout spring roll with a spicy mango dipping sauce, and the seared Ahi tuna with creamy wasabi mashed potatoes. But the goat-cheese wontons with raspberry basil sauce, braised boneless short rib with jalapeño mashed potatoes, and Colorado rack of lamb with pomegranate red-wine sauce ramble in other directions. Happily, everything travels very well together on the plates.

Todd's opens at 4:30pm, in case you've got plans for later.

TIERCE MAJEURE

West of The Strip

WEST OF THE STRIP

Glitter and excitement are spilling over west of The Strip in popular casino resorts and a host of good restaurants (some located in resorts, some freestanding or in little strip malls). The west side is also home to several hotels for budget-minded tourists who don't mind walking the few extra steps to the casinos to lose the money they're saving on lodging. Yet you don't have to go very far west of The Strip to leave it behind completely for the real West. Not half an hour's drive away is **Red Rock Canyon** **National Conservation Area,** the Spring Mountains, and a very different kind of wild from the party on Las Vegas Boulevard.

THE WILDER WEST

There is civilization out here. The suburb of **Summerlin** is one of the area's premier planned communities and home to a performing-arts center, a regional professional dance troupe, two championship golf courses, and enough shopping options to ensure that nobody runs out of upscale trail supplies. But the trails—and the hiking, horseback

Las Vegas News Bureau

riding, camping, rock climbing, etc.—are the real draws out here. Along with the scenery, that is. The 3,000-foot-high, 13-mile-long escarpment at Red Rock Canyon, caused when two geological plates bumped up against each other some 65 million years ago, looks as though a master artist painted bands of gray, red and white along its sandstone facade. Besides the 30 miles of trails, there's a 13-mile scenic driving loop for those who prefer to experience nature in air-conditioned comfort.

At nearby **Spring Mountain Ranch State Park,** you can visit the ranch once owned by Howard Hughes and a campsite used by 19th-century travelers. You can pretend to go back in time and encounter a gunslinger, or join a posse at **Old Nevada**—a re-created 1880s-era mining town on Bonnie Springs Ranch. And if the desert heat begins to be too much for you, head for the wilderness of the Humboldt-Toiyabe National Forest in the **Spring Mountains National Recreation Area.** Mount Charleston, its highest peak at 12,000 feet, is usually 20 to 40 degrees cooler than Las Vegas.

Alizé ✿ (Palms)

Contemporary XXX

106

4321 W. Flamingo Rd.

Phone:	702-951-7000	Dinner daily
Web:	www.alizelv.com	
Prices:	$$$$	

Jeff Green

You'll feel like royalty as the private elevator whisks you from the casino floor up to Alizé's lofty roost at the top of the Palms *(see hotel listing)*. Named for the gentle trade winds that sweep the French Caribbean islands, Alizé affords stunning views of The Strip from its window walls. The chef who brought Andre's to Las Vegas raises the ante at his most luxurious venture by betting on delicious contemporary French cuisine to leave diners hungry to return. Tried-and-true flavor combinations (oven-roasted organic chicken; lobster Thermidor; dessert soufflés) play a solid hand against more contemporary offerings of Kobe beef carpaccio paired with Roma tomato confiture, basil pesto, a spicy-sweet Banyuls reduction and a drizzle of earthy white-truffle oil.

The extensive wine list leaves its heart in France, while it roams the world and comes back to California.

Appetizers	*Entrées*	*Desserts*
● Jumbo Lump Crab Salad	● Muscovy Duck with Peach and Foie Gras Tarte Tatin	● Chocolate or Grand Marnier Soufflé
● Bacon and Black Truffle-crusted Ahi Tuna	● Veal Chop with Artichoke, Morel and Gruyère Cannelloni	● Warm Bilberry Beignets with Apricot Sorbet and Poached Blueberries in Camomile Cream
● Roasted Beet and Goat Cheese Salad	● Colorado Rack of Lamb with Merguez Sausage Crêpe	● Chocolate Fondant

Sharing the nature of infinity

Route du Fort-de-Brégançon - 83250 La Londe-les-Maures - Tél. 33 (0)4 94 01 53 53
Fax 33 (0)4 94 01 53 54 - domaines-ott.com - ott.particuliers@domaines-ott.com

Antonio's (Rio)

Italian ✗✗✗

107

3700 W. Flamingo Rd.

Phone:	702-777-7923	Dinner daily
Web:	www.harrahs.com	
Prices:	$$$	

Rio

If you need a break from the Brazilian *Carnivale* at the Rio *(see hotel listing)*, this serene Italian restaurant in the Ipanema Tower will be *simpatico*. While awaiting your meal, look up to enjoy the view—marble columns support a domed ceiling, painted with a glorious blue sky. Or gaze into an inviting glass of Barolo to get in the mood for the northern-inspired Italian cuisine.

Antonio's isn't a slave to tradition, but interprets it well in dishes like perciatelli with thinly sliced beef tenderloin, candied walnuts and gorgonzola cream. House-cured pancetta wraps around large grilled prawns served with roasted pear tomatoes and broccoli rabe in an artful antipasto. Osso buco isn't the delicate saffron Milanese, but an earthy Tuscan version with wild mushrooms.

Intimate meals in cozy booths and group conviviality in private dining rooms co-exist peacefully here.

Archi's Thai Kitchen

108

6360 W. Flamingo Rd. (at Torrey Pines Dr.)

Phone: 702-880-5550   Lunch & dinner daily
Web: N/A
Prices: 💰

©Mark Gibson

West of The Strip

It's well worth venturing off The Strip to find this little diamond in the rough ("the rough," in this case, is a strip mall), where the kitchen doesn't shy away from making Thai dishes with the traditional amount of spice. At Archi's you can request the degree of heat you desire—from 1 to 10, with 10 bringing tears to your eyes—and the chefs will comply. In spicy basil and tofu, for instance, cubes of firm pan-fried tofu are bathed in chile sauce, and small pieces of hot red chiles are added to turn up the temperature.

Local business types congregate here for the low-priced lunch deals: your choice out of a specified group of entrées served with soup, rice and egg rolls for under $8. At dinner, three different Thai family-style meals range from $22 to $31. If it's something more ambitious you're after, consider the long list of appetizing à la carte fare.

Cafe Wasabi

Japanese ✗

109

7365 W. Sahara Ave. (at Tenaya Way)

Phone:	702-804-9652	Mon – Sat lunch & dinner
Web:	N/A	Sun lunch only
Prices:	$$	

©Mark Gibson

Superior ingredients and skillful sushi chefs make Cafe Wasabi a great place for sushi—at less than half the price you'd pay on The Strip. Forget about theme resorts and over-the-top décor; in this pleasant, modern dining room, which displays a rainbow of hand-blown martini glasses behind the sushi bar, you'll receive a warm welcome from the young staff before you treat your taste buds to some excellent Pacific Rim cuisine.

It's a difficult decision between fusion fare such as miso-glazed salmon with Asian pesto and macadamia-nut rice, and Asian-marinated New York strip steak that shares a plate with pan-fried noodles and baby bok choy. As for sushi, rolls with names like Café Wasabi Lasagna (snow crab, avocado and cream cheese baked in a creamy sauce with sweet soy vinaigrette) will prove intriguing.

A cup of artisan green tea makes a soothing finale.

Ferraro's

Italian

5900 W. Flamingo Rd. (bet Decatur & Jones Blvds.)

Phone: 702-364-5300
Web: www.ferraroslasvegas.com
Prices: $$

Mon – Fri lunch & dinner
Sat dinner only

West of The Strip

Ferraro's

Finally, an off-Strip restaurant that's not located in a strip mall. This stand-alone structure on Flamingo Road welcomes diners with true Italian warmth. That's not surprising, since the elegant eatery has been run by the Ferraro family since 1985.

These days, Mimmo Ferraro (son of founder, Gino) holds the reins in the kitchen. Here he maintains the family's commitment to tradition, serving up the signature osso buco, along with homemade pastas, market-fresh seafood, and *festa* Ferraro for two (a hearty meat sauce made with spare ribs, meatballs and sausage). The wine list sticks mainly to Italy and California, complemented by a nice choice of grappa.

Most of the patrons are regulars, drawn back time and time again by the genial staff, the well-spaced tables and cozy booths, and, of course, the serious cooking. As the family would tell you: *mangia, mangia*.

145

Garduños (Palms)

111

4321 W. Flamingo Rd.

Phone:	866-942-7777	Lunch & dinner daily
Web:	www.palms.com	
Prices:	💰	

©Mark Gibson

Old and New World Mexican fare meld at the Palms *(see hotel listing)* in a cavernous bi-level space embellished with tiled walls, wood beams and artifacts from south of the border. In the center of the main room, the round bar is the place to knock back a round or two of margaritas after a lucrative—or not—day of gambling. The lineup of house margaritas (including drinks blended with fresh fruit, and a "mockarita" for those who prefer their beverages without alcohol) are guaranteed to kick up the party a notch.

Fresh and spicy, Mexican specialties encompass steak *ranchera*, shrimp Diablo, and fire-roasted chicken, in addition to all the standards. Gourmet chili (way beyond Tex-Mex) cites *rojo* (red) and *verde* (green) versions, as well as traditional chicken and pork posole topped with melted cheese and red chile. There's even a children's menu for *los niños*.

West of The Strip

Gaylord India (Rio)

Indian ✗✗

3700 W. Flamingo Rd.

Phone: 702-777-7923
Web: www.playrio.com
Prices: $$

Mon – Fri lunch & dinner
Sat – Sun dinner only

West of The Strip

©Mark Gibson

Established in San Francisco more than 30 years ago, Gaylord has branched out around the Bay Area and other California cities, and now brings its Northern Indian specialties to the Rio *(see hotel listing)*. Two carved wood elephants greet you at the entrance, before you step into the elegant dining space where a courteous young staff takes over.

Respectful of tradition, the kitchen blends its own fresh spices and employs them with a subtle hand. Fragrant dishes such as lamb chop *massala*, chicken *pasanda* (cooked in a mild sauce made with cashews and cream), and, for vegetarians, meatless options like *Burgon Bharta* (eggplant baked with onions, tomatoes and spices). The expansive menu cites a long list of tandoori dishes, curries and biryani rice dishes, as well as fixed-price combinations. Pair your meal with a *lassi*, a frothy yogurt drink served salty or sweet.

Hannah's

West of The Strip

1050 S. Rampart Blvd. (at Charleston Blvd.)

Phone: 702-932-9399   Lunch & dinner daily
Web: www.hannahslv.com
Prices: $$

©Mark Gibson

Poised on the western edge of Las Vegas, the upscale community of Summerlin is where you'll find Hannah An's delightful contribution to the local dining scene. Hannah is the oldest of five daughters born to a well-to-do Vietnamese family who established Thanh Long and Crustacean in San Francisco after being forced to leave their native country in the wake of the Communist invasion in 1975.

At her restaurant in the Boca Park shopping center, An continues her epicurean heritage by skillfully interpreting the family's secret recipes for justly renowned signatures like the pungent and buttery garlic noodles and the pan-roasted Dungeness crab.

With its soothing water features, silk curtains and graceful Asian artwork, Hannah's Zen-like atmosphere proves equally suited to intimate meals for two or group dinners around the communal table.

J.C. Wooloughan
(JW Marriott Resort)

Gastropub ✗

114

221 N. Rampart Blvd. (at Summerlin Pkwy.)

Phone: 702-869-7725   Lunch & dinner daily
Web: www.jwlasvegasresort.com
Prices: ⊜⊜

JW Marriott

A visit to this oh-so-Irish pub in the JW Marriott Resort *(see hotel listing)* is like taking a trip to the Emerald Isle. In fact, the entire place was designed and built outside Dublin, then taken apart, shipped across the Pond and reassembled in Las Vegas.

True to form, Wooloughan's menu includes a good selection of Irish whiskey and ale, but the real attraction here is the generous portions of pub food. Order up a pint while you ponder the menu; shepherd's pie crowned with a thick layer of "champ" (mashed potatoes) makes a hearty meal, but bangers 'n' mash or crispy fish 'n' chips (cod dipped in the house ale batter) are also tempting and authentic treats.

Finish up with the dense and delicious, syrup-saturated cake known as sticky toffee pudding, and you'll find yourself nostalgic for the Old Sod—whether or not you're Irish.

Marc's

Italian ✗✗

115

7290 W. Lake Mead Blvd. (at Tenaya Way)

Phone:	702-562-1921	Mon – Fri lunch & dinner
Web:	www.marcsrestaurant.com	Sat – Sun dinner only
Prices:	$$	

Marc's Italian Steakhouse

The corner of a modern shopping strip marks the spot of this casual, neighborhood Italian restaurant. In the dining room, black linens cover the tables and booths line two side walls; outside, a patio faces the parking lot.

It's the generous servings of simple home-style Italian fare, not the décor, that keep locals coming back for more. Billing itself as an "Italian steakhouse," Marc's features a selection of prime steaks and Provimi veal. But tradition wouldn't be honored without the likes of eggplant parmesan, *pasta fagiola*, and wood-oven-roasted pizzas spread with velvety tomato sauce and finished off with such toppings as wild mushrooms or grilled basil chicken. References to the Rat Pack pepper the menu in Penne alla Dean Martin and Chicken Sinatra.

A more spirited menu touts a selection of martinis, perhaps another Rat Pack holdover.

N9NE (Palms)

Steakhouse

116

4321 W. Flamingo Rd.

Phone: 702-933-9900 Dinner daily
Web: www.n9negroup.com
Prices: $$$$

N9NE

With a hip vibe that would rival any in South Beach, N9NE burst upon the Vegas scene when the Palms resort *(see hotel listing)* opened in 2001. Chic chocolate suede booths and glittering columns that reflect the room's changing colored lights raise the stakes in this restaurant-cum-nightclub, frequented by as glamorous a crowd as you'll find anywhere in town.

Whether you go to see or be seen, don't miss out on the main attraction: prime aged steaks and chops. Perfectly seared and full of flavor, the meat is excellent by itself, or paired with Alaskan King crab legs or a Maine lobster tail and white-truffle aïoli as surf and turf.

This hotspot is part of the N9NE Group, founded in Chicago by Scott de Graff and Michael Morton. As the son of Arnie Morton—who founded the eponymous Chicago steakhouse chain—the latter partner comes by his calling naturally.

Nora's Cuisine

117

Italian

6020 W. Flamingo Rd. (at Jones Blvd.)

Phone: 702-365-6713
Web: www.norascuisine.com
Prices:

Mon – Fri lunch & dinner
Sat dinner only

©Mark Gibson

Yes, Virginia, there is a Nora in the kitchen here, and she cooks up tasty and traditional Italian comfort food with Sicilian accents. Nora Mauro and her husband, Gino, launched this restaurant in 1991. Since then, thanks to several additions to the space (including a popular sports bar), they've mushroomed from a humble seating capacity of 12 to room for 300 diners.

Local business folks and families appreciate the brick-oven-fired pizzas and hefty portions of perpetual favorites like "crazy" alfredo (with chicken, sausage, shrimp, mushrooms, roasted bell peppers, sun-dried tomatoes and jalapeños added to the classic recipe), and breaded and roasted pork tenderloin *alla Siciliana*.

The ambience is unpretentious, the service fast and furious, and the room packed with a casual crowd of regulars who prefer to keep this place to themselves.

Nove Italiano (Palms)

118

4321 W. Flamingo Rd.

Phone: 702-942-6800   Dinner daily
Web: www.n9negroup.com
Prices: **$$$**

West of The Strip

Nove Italiano

Nove ("nine" in Italian) makes a fitting moniker for the N9NE Groups' sexy addition to the new 53-story Fantasy Tower at the Palms resort *(see hotel listing)*. From the restaurant's 51st-floor roost (one floor below the new Playboy Club) you'll have a great view of The Strip, not to mention the Travertine marble floor and Swarovski crystal chandeliers that outfit the dining room to the nines.

Service remains surprisingly attentive, despite the booming club music and the glamorous partyers who gather in boisterous groups—this is not the place for a quiet meal. It is the place to savor well-executed Northern and Southern Italian fare, along with an A-list of varietals that struts its stuff from all the major wine-making regions of Italy.

Dress to impress for a dinner here, and plan to linger in the seductive lounge, which is extended by airy terraces.

Ping Pang Pong (Gold Coast)

Chinese ✕

West of The Strip

4000 W. Flamingo Rd.

Phone: 702-247-8136

Web: www.goldcoastcasino.com

Prices: 💰💰

Lunch & dinner daily

Ping Pang Pong

It's an intriguing name, suggesting a one-off table-tennis game to English-speakers, but the food here is no joke. Housed inside the unpretentious Gold Coast Hotel, this popular place spotlights specialties from the diverse provinces of China. The menu wanders through noodles and rice to clay pot dishes and congee, and from tea-smoked duck to whole steamed fish. It's quite a broad selection, including "Provincial Favorites" like Cantonese pulled chicken and double-braised scallop hot pot.

At lunchtime, locals flock here for dim sum. During this lively feast, Chinese waitresses make their rounds with trays of aromatic meat dumplings, spicy black-bean chicken feet, abalone puff pastry and much, much more.

Besides good food, Ping Pang Pong represents a great bargain. Either a dim sum lunch or an average three-course dinner will cost you just shy of $25.

Rosemary's

120

8125 W. Sahara Ave. (bet. Buffalo Dr. & Cimarron Rd.)

Phone:	702-869-2251	Mon – Fri lunch & dinner
Web:	www.rosemarysrestaurant.com	Sat – Sun dinner only
Prices:	$$	

West of The Strip

Rosemary's Restaurant

Michael Jordan (the chef, not the star basketball player of New York City steakhouse fame) and his wife, Wendy, take advantage of their time spent working in New Orleans to infuse Rosemary's contemporary cuisine with Southern accents. The likes of Creole-seared King salmon, grilled chicken breast on a bed of hoppin' John, and Hugo's Texas BBQ shrimp show their talents—and their carefully selected products—to best advantage.

Opened in 1999, Rosemary's consistently wins raves with locals and tourists who venture to this strip mall off The Strip in search of fine cuisine in a low-key family atmosphere. Locals in the know go for the three-course prix-fixe lunch—which offers a lot of bang for 25 bucks—or the nightly carry-out specials. And on Sunday night, Rosemary's offers half-price bottles of wine—where on The Strip can you find a deal like that?

Shizen (JW Marriott Resort)

121

Japanese 🍴

221 N. Rampart Blvd. (at Summerlin Pkwy.)

Phone: 702-869-7900
Web: www.jwlasvegasresort.com
Prices: $$

Dinner daily

JW Marriott

Tired of high-priced food on The Strip? Take a ride out to Summerlin, and you'll find fresh Japanese cuisine at modest prices at the JW Marriott Las Vegas Resort *(see hotel listing)*.

Dining takes on three distinct forms here. First, there's the semi-circular sushi bar where the chefs slice up specialty items like the Volcano Roll (minced tuna mixed with chile sauce and topped with slices of fatty, white albacore tuna) and assorted sushi and sashimi. Then there's the dining area, where guests can order off the à la carte menu; the broiled misoyaki butterfish, marinated in sweet miso and salty soy sauce, is a perennial favorite. Last, but far from least, are the *teppan yaki* tables, for which Shizen is locally prized. Here, chefs with a flair for showmanship prepare your meal on large, flat-top grills. So many choices, so little time.

Terra Rossa (Red Rock Resort)

Italian ✕✕

11011 W. Charleston Blvd. (at I-215)

Lunch & dinner daily

Phone: 702-797-7576
Web: www.redrocklasvegas.com
Prices: $$

Station Casinos

West of The Strip

Located about ten miles from The Strip, Red Rock Resort *(see hotel listing)* capitalizes on its proximity to the area's natural beauty, specifically Red Rock Canyon. Even the resort's Italian restaurant echoes the red rocks in its name.

The beige tones, polished wood and marble accents in Terra Rossa's dining room don't distract from the food, which is well-prepared and flavorful. "Italian" here means generous portions of arugula salad tossed in a parmesan-lemon vinaigrette, traditional pastas, pizzas cooked in the wood-burning-oven, and main courses like *gamberoni Fra Diavolo* (tail-on prawns served in a spicy tomato sauce) or veal *alla fiorentina* (a grilled 14-ounce veal Porterhouse, served with potatoes and caponata).

Friendly service and a casual-chic atmosphere add to the tasty cuisine to make this place a favorite of both hotel guests and locals.

Thai Spice

Nita Kittypong

West of The Strip

Thai 🍴

4433 W. Flamingo Rd. (at Arville St.)

Phone: 702-362-5308
Web: N/A
Prices: 💰💰

Lunch & dinner daily

There are restaurants you go to for the atmosphere and restaurants you go to for the cuisine; Thai Spice is one of the latter. Set in a little shopping center a block away from the Palms hotel and easily accessible from The Strip, this unassuming spot consistently wins local raves for its authentic and inexpensive Thai dishes.

A creamy peanut dressing seasons a vegetable salad, while the house version of pad Thai contains chicken and shrimp enlivened by ground chile pepper. Make sure to tell the pleasant Asian waitstaff how spicy you like your food, and note that "medium spicy" to most American palates results in a pretty piquant Thai interpretation. (Fiery dishes are indicated on the menu with an asterisk.)

Desserts are limited, but if it's offered, the sweet coconut custard will help mellow any residual heat from your meal.

Innovation has good prospects whenever it is cleaner, safer and more efficient.

The MICHELIN Energy green tire lasts 25% longer*.
It also provides fuel savings of 2 to 3%
while reducing CO_2 emissions.

* on average compared to competing tires in the same category.

Downtown

DOWNTOWN LAS VEGAS

Although the "other" Las Vegas often gets overlooked in favor of the famed Strip of Las Vegas Boulevard, Downtown is where the seeds of glitz and glamour that now define the city first sprouted.

LET THERE BE LIGHT— NEON, THAT IS

When the humble railroad post of Las Vegas was incorporated as a city in March 1911, the Downtown spine of Fremont Street was an unlikely party center since bars were forbidden along it. The thoroughfare livened up as would-be bar owners figured out they could get liquor licenses by opening hotels—often with very few rooms. Legalized gambling juiced things up further in 1931 when The Northern Club got the first Nevada gaming license. By the 40s, casino-lined Fremont Street was a neon "Glitter Gulch." But not until 1946, the same year that the iconic 48-foot-tall neon cowboy named Vegas Vic rose over the Pioneer Club, did the Golden Nugget become Fremont's first building constructed as a casino.

ALL THE GLITTERS

Vic's still there, but the Nugget's original sign lies in the Neon

©Mark Gibson

160

Museum—a casualty of Steve Wynn's 1980s-era renovation. Wynn started The Strip's mega-resort renaissance as civic leaders in the 90s pondered how to keep Glitter Gulch aglow. The **Fremont Street Experience**, a nightly light (some 16 million) and sound extravaganza was the answer. The five-block pedestrian zone now boasts 10 casinos, more than 60 restaurants, and too many bars to count. Third Street, particularly, is a hotspot for trendy bistros and bars.

Downtown's serious side centers on a booming business and government center. In 2005, the **Las Vegas Market** opened as a state-of-the-art exhibit space for the retail furniture and design trade. Plans continue for the 12-million-square-foot **World Market Center**, which will encompass exhibit space in 8 buildings on 57 contiguous acres downtown. When completed in 2012, the center will combine all segments of the industry on one mega-campus. Also in the works is the 61-acre Union Park development with proposed medical and performing-arts centers, highrises and the World Jewelry Center. The Arts Factory on Charleston Boulevard now anchors a thriving **Arts District**. Flashiest of all perhaps is still Vegas Vic, who waves, winks and welcomes visitors as he has for six decades.

Andre's ✿

French ✗✗

401 S. 6th St. (bet. Bridger & Clark Aves.)

Phone: 702-385-5016
Web: www.andrelv.com
Prices: $$$$

Mon – Sat dinner only

Downtown

Tomas Muscionico

Long before Las Vegas claimed a constellation of star chefs, Andre's was the city's special-occasion restaurant. Tucked away on a quiet residential street, this 1930s-era home has been transformed into a warm, French provincial setting incorporating dark, exposed ceiling beams, rough plaster walls and walnut wainscoting, with bottles from local icon and chef/owner André Rochat's private collection of Cognac and Armagnac displayed in the front reception and bar areas.

French cuisine here excels in classicism, restraint and formality. Rich flavors abound in preparations such as a wonderfully caramelized roasted rack of lamb with lamb ravioli and earthy brown lentils wrapped in green cabbage leaves; or a silky, black-truffle-studded terrine of duck foie gras that melts in your mouth. For dessert, a fluffy Grand Marnier soufflé will guarantee you sweet dreams.

Appetizers
- Andre's Scampi Served in a Puff Pastry Shell
- Coquille St. Jacques in a Vermouth Cream Sauce with Hollandaise Glaçage
- Phyllo-wrapped Baked Anjou Pear and Roquefort Cheese

Entrées
- Dover Sole Sautéed Véronique or Poached Léon de Lyon
- Sautéed Filet of Beef au Poivre
- Sautéed Veal Chop with Morels and Sorrel Agnolotti

Desserts
- Chocolate or Grand Marnier Soufflé
- Tarte Tatin
- Profiteroles

Casa Don Juan

125

1204 S. Main St. (at California St.)

Phone: 702-384-8070
Web: N/A
Prices: 💶

Lunch & dinner daily

Downtown

©Mark Gibson

Take a break from run-of-the-mill steakhouses in the hub of Las Vegas at this cheery Mexican restaurant. Local business people, families and other Downtown denizens frequent Casa Don Juan not only for its sunny atmosphere and friendly, efficient service, but also for its copious portions of good Mexican food.

Simple and moderately spiced, the cuisine here runs to standards like enchiladas, tacos and tostadas. Huge burritos—a meal in themselves—come with sides of tomato-scented Mexican rice and refried beans. Tasty fish tacos are made with a mild white fish fillet folded inside a soft white-corn tortilla along with fresh pico de gallo and a generous scoop of creamy guacamole.

Don Juan, with its colorful piñatas hanging above the tiki-hut-inspired bar, makes a festive option for a midday meal in an area largely lacking in good places for lunch.

Grotto (Golden Nugget)

Italian ✕

129 E. Fremont St. (at 1st St.)

Phone: 702-386-8341

Web: www.grottorestaurants.com

Prices: $$

Lunch & dinner daily

Downtown

Golden Nugget

As the first luxury hotel to open in Las Vegas (1946), the Golden Nugget has undergone a lot of changes over the years. The most recent renovations, made in 2006, included the addition of Grotto Ristorante.

A casual Italian trattoria, Grotto is located just past the lobby reception area, where it sits slightly raised above the casino floor. Here, diners enjoy a view of the new $30-million pool, which includes a 200,000-gallon shark tank. If memories of *Jaws* make you squeamish, turn your attention to the exhibition pizza oven and antipasti station, where you can watch chefs prepare something for you to eat, instead of watching something that might fancy eating you.

Prompt, cordial service, and heaping plates of homemade pastas, thin-crust pizzas, and meat and fish entrées make this roomy restaurant a winner with families, groups and hotel guests alike.

Vic & Anthony's (Golden Nugget)

127

129 E. Fremont St. (at 1st St.)

Phone:	702-386-8399	Sat – Thu dinner only
Web:	www.vicandanthonys.com	Fri lunch & dinner
Prices:	$$$	

Downtown

Golden Nugget

Downtown Las Vegas is steakhouse central, where every hotel seems to claim a restaurant honoring meat in its many forms. Vic & Anthony's fits the mold with its dark, clubby atmosphere, full of wood paneling, leather chairs and candlelight.

Your satisfaction is the staff's command here. When servers bring your steak to the table, they will request that you cut into it to make sure that the meat is cooked to your liking. Who wouldn't like a juicy filet mignon, perfectly seared until the outside is crisp and the inside is tender and moist? Or an appetizer of maple-glazed quail, sticky-sweet and deep brown, and drizzled with spicy Sriracha sauce made from ground chile, garlic and vinegar? Of course, lobster and a few other seafood choices make their required appearance.

Dining alone? Don't let all the couples intimidate you; the full menu is available at the bar.

Michelin Now Has Fitments Approved By Harley-Davidson.

Since 1889, Michelin has been dedicated to building innovation and quality into every tire we make. So it's hardly surprising that Harley-Davidson® has approved Michelin® Commander® and Macadam® 50 tires for use on many popular models of America's oldest and most respected motorcycle brand. Michelin translates its vast racing experience into riding confidence and performance, helping Harley-Davidson motorcycle owners to maximize their riding enjoyment. It's a better way forward. Consult your Harley-Davidson dealer for complete information on approved Michelin tire fitments.

MICHELIN
A better way forward

Where to **stay**

Alphabetical list of Hotels

Where to stay

Bellagio

001

3600 Las Vegas Blvd. S. (at Flamingo Rd.)

Phone: 702-693-7111 or 888-987-3456
Fax: 702-693-8555
Web: www.bellagio.com
Prices: $$$

3421 Rooms

512 Suites

Inspired by the Italian village of Bellagio on the shores of Lake Como, Steve Wynn's *bellisimo* resort changed the face of The Strip in 1998. Wynn sunk $1.6 billion into his gargantuan hotel (now owned by the MGM Mirage group), which fronts an 8-acre lake famed for its fountain and light shows.

In the lobby, Dale Chihuly's breathtaking sculpture *Fiori di Como* blooms across the ceiling in a rainbow of some 2,000 hand-blown glass flowers. The real flora, however, bursts into view in the nearby Conservatory, where a striking display of plants change with the season.

Bellagio guests choose their accommodations among a staggering 3,421 spacious rooms and 512 suites appointed in European elegance with luxe bedding and large bathrooms with a soaking tub and separate shower. Buttons on a panel by the bed will turn off the lights and close the curtains—all you have to do is lift a finger.

The Strip

MGM Mirage

Where to eat...

The Strip

BELLAGIO

CASINO LEVEL

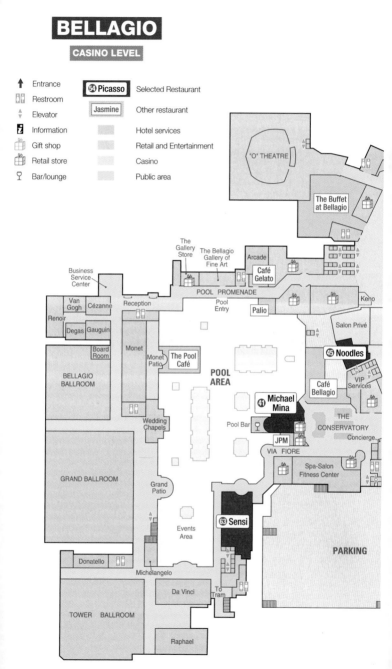

↑	Entrance
	Restroom
	Elevator
	Information
	Gift shop
	Retail store
	Bar/lounge

54 Picasso	Selected Restaurant
Jasmine	Other restaurant
	Hotel services
	Retail and Entertainment
	Casino
	Public area

"O" THEATRE

The Buffet at Bellagio

The Gallery Store

The Bellagio Gallery of Fine Art

Arcade

Café Gelato

Business Service Center

POOL PROMENADE

Van Gogh

Cézanne

Reception

Pool Entry

Palio

Keno

Renoir

Degas

Gauguin

Salon Privé

Board Room

Monet

Monet Patio

The Pool Café

POOL AREA

45 Noodles

BELLAGIO BALLROOM

Café Bellagio

VIP Services

41 Michael Mina

THE CONSERVATORY

Wedding Chapels

Pool Bar

Concierge

JPM

VIA FIORE

GRAND BALLROOM

Spa-Salon Fitness Center

Grand Patio

Events Area

63 Sensi

PARKING

Donatello

Michelangelo

To Tram

Da Vinci

TOWER BALLROOM

Raphael

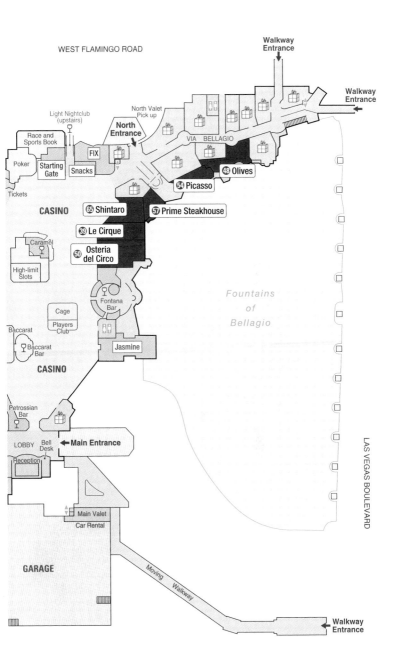

WEST FLAMINGO ROAD

Walkway Entrance

Walkway Entrance

Light Nightclub (upstairs)

North Valet Pick up

North Entrance

VIA BELLAGIO

Race and Sports Book

Poker

Starting Gate

FIX

Snacks

Tickets

48 Olives

54 Picasso

CASINO

65 Shintaro

57 Prime Steakhouse

39 Le Cirque

Caramêl

50 Osteria del Circo

High-limit Slots

Fountains of Bellagio

Cage

Players Club

Fontana Bar

Baccarat

Baccarat Bar

CASINO

Jasmine

Petrossian Bar

LOBBY

Bell Desk

← **Main Entrance**

Reception

LAS VEGAS BOULEVARD

Main Valet

Car Rental

GARAGE

Moving Walkway

Walkway Entrance

173

Caesars Palace

002

3570 Las Vegas Blvd S. (at Flamingo Rd.)

Phone:	702-731-7110 or 866-227-5938
Fax:	702-967-3890
Web:	www.caesarspalace.com
Prices:	$$$

1834 Rooms

1504 Suites

Friends, Romans, Countrymen ... there's room for everyone in this Greco-Roman extravaganza, which tops out with more than 3,300 rooms and suites strewn between five palatial towers. Set on 85 acres in the middle of The Strip, Caesars Palace reigns over 26 restaurants, 5 nightclubs, 6 wedding chapels, 4 heated outdoor swimming pools, 3 casinos, 24,000 square feet of meeting space, acres of designer shops, and a 4,100-seat Colosseum that books a steady stream of big-name headliners.

Immense fountains, gigantic statues, and soaring marble columns define the classical architecture inside and out. Opened in 1966, the resort has since racked up more than $1 billion in renovations, most recently adding a 50,000-square-foot spa, and the new Augustus Tower, whose luxurious rooms are appointed with a fax machine, flat-screen TVs, and marble baths. All hail, Caesars.

The Strip

Caesars Palace

Where to eat...

▶ *Recommended*

▶ *Also*

The Strip

CAESARS PALACE

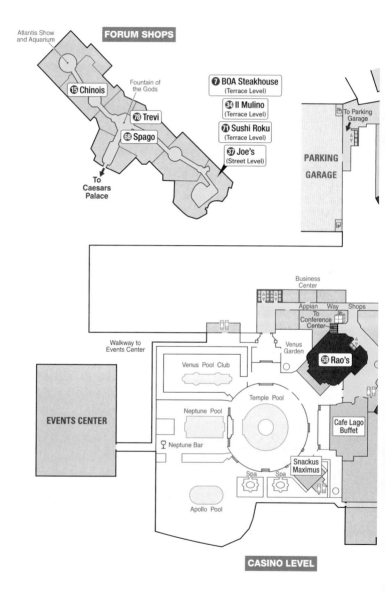

FORUM SHOPS

Atlantis Show and Aquarium

15 Chinois

Fountain of the Gods

78 Trevi

68 Spago

To Caesars Palace

7 BOA Steakhouse (Terrace Level)

34 Il Mulino (Terrace Level)

71 Sushi Roku (Terrace Level)

37 Joe's (Street Level)

To Parking Garage

PARKING GARAGE

Business Center

Appian Way Shops

To Conference Center

Walkway to Events Center

Venus Garden

58 Rao's

Venus Pool Club

Temple Pool

Neptune Pool

EVENTS CENTER

Neptune Bar

Cafe Lago Buffet

Snackus Maximus

Spa   Spa

Apollo Pool

CASINO LEVEL

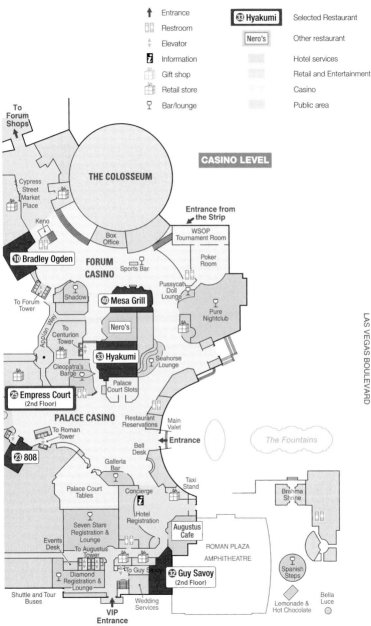

Entrance
Restroom
Elevator
Information
Gift shop
Retail store
Bar/lounge

33 Hyakumi — Selected Restaurant

Nero's — Other restaurant

Hotel services
Retail and Entertainment
Casino
Public area

CASINO LEVEL

To Forum Shops

THE COLOSSEUM

Cypress Street Market Place

Keno

Box Office

Entrance from the Strip

WSOP Tournament Room

Poker Room

10 Bradley Ogden

FORUM CASINO

Sports Bar

Pussycat Doll Lounge

Pure Nightclub

Shadow

40 Mesa Grill

To Forum Tower

Nero's

To Centurion Tower

Seahorse Lounge

33 Hyakumi

Cleopatra's Barge

Palace Court Slots

25 Empress Court (2nd Floor)

PALACE CASINO

Restaurant Reservations

Main Valet

Entrance

The Fountains

To Roman Tower

Bell Desk

23 808

Galleria Bar

Taxi Stand

Brahma Shrine

Palace Court Tables

Concierge

Hotel Registration

Seven Stars Registration & Lounge

Augustus Cafe

ROMAN PLAZA AMPHITHEATRE

Events Desk

To Augustus Tower

To Guy Savoy

42 Guy Savoy (2nd Floor)

Spanish Steps

Diamond Registration & Lounge

Shuttle and Tour Buses

Wedding Services

Lemonade & Hot Chocolate

Bella Luce

VIP Entrance

Applan Way

LAS VEGAS BOULEVARD

FLAMINGO ROAD

Mandalay Bay

003

3950 Las Vegas Blvd. S. (at Mandalay Bay Rd.)

Phone: 702-632-7777 or 877-632-7000
Fax: 702-891-7270
Web: www.mandalaybay.com
Prices: $$$

2351 Rooms

440 Suites

With more than 4,000 rooms between the original hotel and connecting properties THEhotel and The Four Seasons, you can take your pick of themes at Mandalay Bay. Rooms in the original resort—which encompasses an 11-acre beach with 2,700 tons of real sand—retain the South Seas look with tropical florals and animal prints. His-and-hers closets and featherbeds kick up the comfort.

Next door, the 43-story tower called THEhotel caters to the young and the hip with its bold, contemporary décor and spacious suites. Both business and leisure guests enjoy the wet bar, the 42-inch plasma TV, and the copier/fax/printer that come in each suite. Known for its impeccable service, The Four Seasons occupies floors 35 to 39 of Mandalay Bay, adding another 424 elegant rooms to the mix.

Need chic attire for lounging at one of the resort's three pools? Head for Mandalay Place shopping arcade.

The Strip

MGM Mirage

Where to eat...

▶ *RECOMMENDED*

Aureole ✿	✗✗✗	29
Border Grill	✗✗	33
Charlie Palmer Steak (Four Seasons)	✗✗✗	38
China Grill	✗✗	39
Fleur de Lys	✗✗✗	53
miX (THEhotel) ✿	✗✗✗	67
The Noodle Shop	✗	71
rm seafood	✗✗✗	85
rumjungle	✗✗	86
Stripsteak	✗✗	95
Trattoria del Lupo	✗✗	102
Verandah (Four Seasons)	✗✗✗	105

▶ *ALSO*

House of Blues
Red Square
Red, White and Blue
Shanghai Lilly

The Strip

179

MANDALAY BAY

CASINO LEVEL

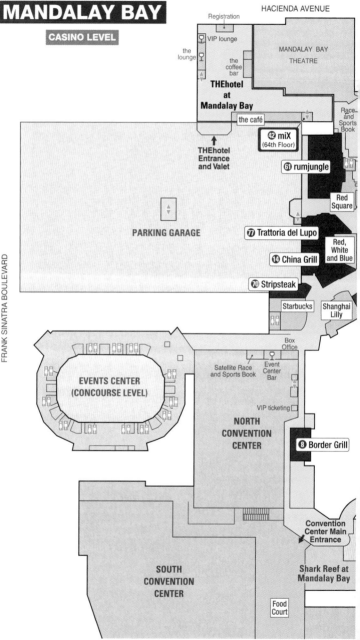

HACIENDA AVENUE

Registration

VIP lounge

the lounge

MANDALAY BAY THEATRE

the coffee bar

THEhotel at Mandalay Bay

the café

Race and Sports Book

42 miX (64th Floor)

61 rumjungle

THEhotel Entrance and Valet

Red Square

PARKING GARAGE

77 Trattoria del Lupo

Red, White and Blue

14 China Grill

70 Stripsteak

Starbucks

Shanghai Lilly

FRANK SINATRA BOULEVARD

Box Office

EVENTS CENTER (CONCOURSE LEVEL)

Satellite Race and Sports Book

Event Center Bar

VIP ticketing

NORTH CONVENTION CENTER

8 Border Grill

SOUTH CONVENTION CENTER

Convention Center Main Entrance

Shark Reef at Mandalay Bay

Food Court

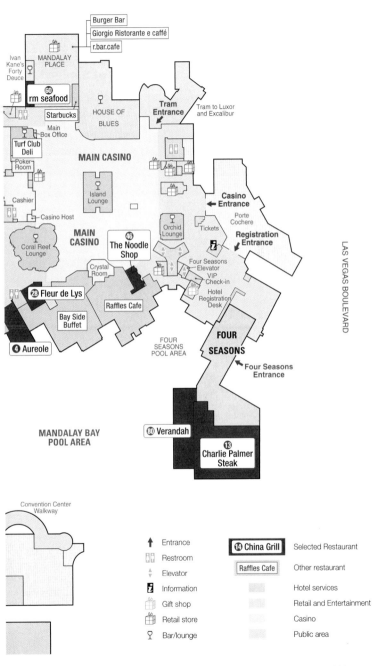

Burger Bar
Giorgio Ristorante e caffé
r.bar.cafe

Ivan Kane's Forty Deuce

MANDALAY PLACE

60 rm seafood

Starbucks

HOUSE OF BLUES

Tram Entrance

Tram to Luxor and Excalibur

Main Box Office

Turf Club Deli

Poker Room

MAIN CASINO

Cashier

Casino Host

Island Lounge

Casino Entrance

Porte Cochere

Orchid Lounge

Tickets

Registration Entrance

MAIN CASINO

Coral Reef Lounge

46 The Noodle Shop

Four Seasons Elevator

VIP Check-in

Crystal Room

28 Fleur de Lys

Raffles Cafe

Hotel Registration Desk

Bay Side Buffet

4 Aureole

FOUR SEASONS POOL AREA

FOUR SEASONS

Four Seasons Entrance

MANDALAY BAY POOL AREA

80 Verandah

13 Charlie Palmer Steak

LAS VEGAS BOULEVARD

Convention Center Walkway

↑ Entrance

🛗 Restroom

↕ Elevator

ℹ Information

🎁 Gift shop

🎁 Retail store

♀ Bar/lounge

14 China Grill — Selected Restaurant

Raffles Cafe — Other restaurant

Hotel services

Retail and Entertainment

Casino

Public area

MGM Grand

004

3799 Las Vegas Blvd. S. (at Tropicana Ave.)

Phone:	702-891-7777 or 877-880-0880
Fax:	702-891-3036
Web:	www.mgmgrand.com
Prices:	$$$

4293
Rooms

751
Suites

With more than 5,000 rooms and suites, the MGM Grand ranks as one of the largest hotels in Las Vegas. The green-glass behemoth rises 30 stories, its entrance guarded by a 100,000-pound bronze statue of the MGM mascot. The leonine theme continues inside at the glass-enclosed Lion Habitat—one of the few things in town you don't have to pay for.

This resort roars with entertainment opportunities, including the Cirque de Soleil show KÀ, and 16,800 seats for megaconcerts and championship boxing in the Grand Garden Arena. Not to mention a menu of celebrity chefs including Joël Robuchon, Tom Colicchio, Michael Mina and Wolfgang Puck.

Standard rooms are large and comfortable, while renovated West Wing rooms say luxury with feather beds and sleek granite baths. For high-rollers, the Tony Chi-designed Skylofts feature commodious floorplans, stunning views, and 24-hour butler service.

The Strip

MGM Mirage

Where to eat...

► *Recommended*

► *Also*

Rainforest Café
'wichcraft
Wolfgang Puck Bar & Grill

The Strip

MGM GRAND

CASINO LEVEL

↑ Entrance

🛁 Restroom

↕ Elevator

ℹ Information

🎁 Gift shop

🏬 Retail store

🍷 Bar/lounge

㉔ Emeril's Selected Restaurant

Studio Café Other restaurant

Hotel services

Retail and Entertainment

Casino

Public area

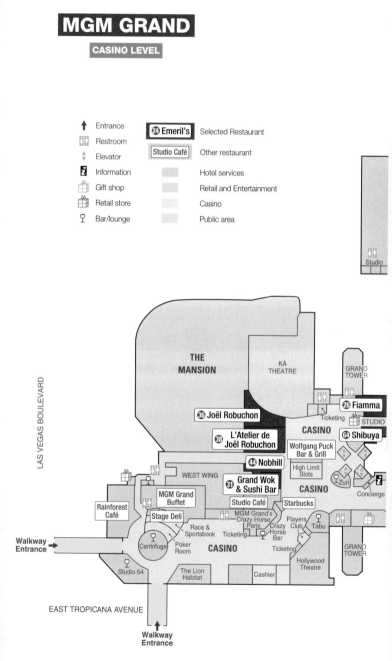

THE MANSION

KÀ THEATRE

GRAND TOWER

Studio

㉖ Fiamma

Ticketing

STUDIO

CASINO

㉞ Joël Robuchon

㊿ Shibuya

㊳ L'Atelier de Joël Robuchon

Wolfgang Puck Bar & Grill

㊽ Nobhill

High Limit Slots

CASINO

WEST WING

㉛ Grand Wok & Sushi Bar

Zuri

Concierge

MGM Grand Buffet

Studio Café

Starbucks

Rainforest Café

Stage Deli

MGM Grand's Crazy Horse Paris

Players Club

Tabu

Race & Sportsbook

Ticketing

Crazy Horse Bar

Centrifuge

Poker Room

CASINO

Ticketing

GRAND TOWER

Walkway Entrance

Hollywood Theatre

Studio 54

The Lion Habitat

Cashier

LAS VEGAS BOULEVARD

EAST TROPICANA AVENUE

Walkway Entrance

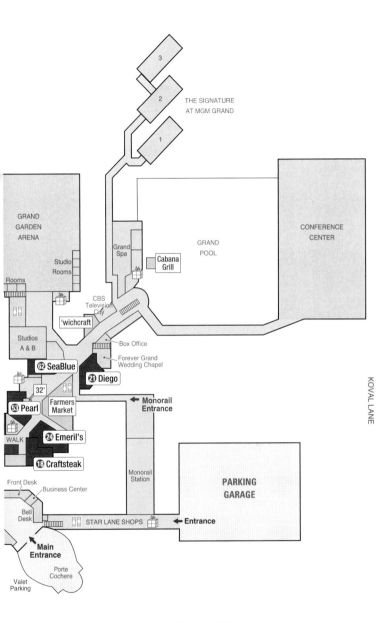

3

2

1

THE SIGNATURE
AT MGM GRAND

GRAND
GARDEN
ARENA

CONFERENCE
CENTER

Studio
Rooms

Grand
Spa

GRAND
POOL

Rooms

Cabana
Grill

CBS
Television
City

'wichcraft

Box Office

Studios
A & B

Forever Grand
Wedding Chapel

62 SeaBlue

21 Diego

32"

← Monorail
Entrance

53 Pearl

Farmers
Market

WALK

24 Emeril's

18 Craftsteak

Monorail
Station

PARKING
GARAGE

KOVAL LANE

Front Desk

Business Center

Bell
Desk

STAR LANE SHOPS

← Entrance

Main
Entrance

Porte
Cochere

Valet
Parking

EAST TROPICANA AVENUE

Mirage

005

3400 Las Vegas Blvd. S.
(bet. Flamingo Rd. & Spring Mountain Rd.)

Phone: 702-791-7111 or 800-627-6667
Fax: 702-791-7446
Web: www.mirage.com
Prices: $$

2763
Rooms

281
Suites

No, you're not seeing things; there is a volcano spewing fiery lava 50 feet in the air in a 3-acre lagoon on Las Vegas Boulevard. Welcome to the Mirage.

A dowager on The Strip, the Mirage opened in 1989, leading off the city's boom of themed megaresorts in the 1990s. She may look a bit less glamorous now, eclipsed by newer neighbors The Venetian and Wynn, but this lady is no tramp.

Inside, palm trees, bright orchids and cascading waterfalls fill a skylit space with the sights and sounds of the tropics. Rooms were redone in 2002, in sunny yellows or earth tones and botanical prints. Measuring 400 square feet, deluxe accommodations boast marble entryways and baths, and enjoy a view of The Strip or the lush pool area.

For entertainment, the Cirque de Soleil production Love™—which debuted in 2006—is set to Beatles tunes, and impersonator Danny Gans holds sway in his own theater.

The Strip

MGM Mirage

Where to eat...

▶ *RECOMMENDED*

Fin	ⅩⅩ	52
STACK	ⅩⅩ	94

▶ *ALSO*

Carnegie Delicatessen
Cravings Buffet
Japonais
Kokomo's
Onda
Samba

The Strip

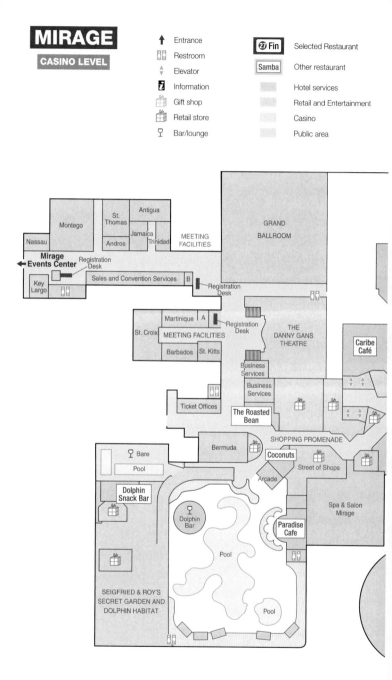

MIRAGE
CASINO LEVEL

↑ Entrance
🚻 Restroom
↕ Elevator
ℹ️ Information
🎁 Gift shop
🏬 Retail store
🍷 Bar/lounge

🌀 Fin — Selected Restaurant
Samba — Other restaurant
Hotel services
Retail and Entertainment
Casino
Public area

Nassau
Montego
St. Thomas
Antigua
Jamaica
Andros
Trinidad
MEETING FACILITIES
GRAND BALLROOM

Mirage Events Center
Registration Desk
Key Largo
Sales and Convention Services
B
Registration Desk

St. Croix
Martinique
A
Registration Desk
MEETING FACILITIES
Barbados
St. Kitts
THE DANNY GANS THEATRE
Caribe Café

Business Services
Business Services
Ticket Offices
The Roasted Bean

SHOPPING PROMENADE

Bermuda
Coconuts
Street of Shops
Arcade

🍷 Bare
Pool
Dolphin Snack Bar
🍷 Dolphin Bar
Pool
Paradise Cafe
Spa & Salon Mirage

SEIGFRIED & ROY'S SECRET GARDEN AND DOLPHIN HABITAT
Pool

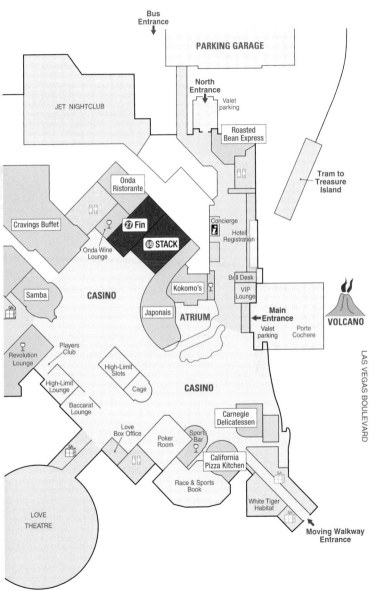

Bus
Entrance
↓

PARKING GARAGE

North
Entrance
↓

Valet
parking

JET NIGHTCLUB

Roasted
Bean Express

Tram to
Treasure
Island

Onda
Ristorante

Concierge

Cravings Buffet

27 Fin

Hotel
Registration

59 STACK

Onda Wine
Lounge

Bell Desk

Kokomo's

VIP
Lounge

Samba

CASINO

Japonais

ATRIUM

Main
Entrance
←

VOLCANO

Valet
parking

Porte
Cochere

Players
Club

Revolution
Lounge

CASINO

High-Limit
Slots

High-Limit
Lounge

Cage

LAS VEGAS BOULEVARD

Baccarat
Lounge

Carnegie
Delicatessen

Love
Box Office

Poker
Room

Sports
Bar

California
Pizza Kitchen

Race & Sports
Book

White Tiger
Habitat

LOVE
THEATRE

Moving Walkway
Entrance

Paris

006

3655 Las Vegas Blvd. S. (bet. Flamingo Rd. & Harmon Ave.)

Phone: 702-946-7000 or 877-796-2096
Fax: 702-946-4405
Web: www.parislasvegas.com
Prices: $$

2621
Rooms

295
Suites

From the Eiffel Tower to the sidewalk cafe, Paris Las Vegas is as French as you can get—on this side of the Pond, anyway. The observation deck on the 50-story scale model of the *Tour Eiffel* may overlook the neon of The Strip, but when you see the Arc de Triomphe and the façades of the Louvre, the Opéra and the Hôtel de Ville below, it's easy to pretend you're in the real City of Light.

Joie de vivre oozes from every pore of this resort, beginning with the lobby, dripping with gilt trim and glittering crystal chandeliers. French ballads croon in the elevator as you are whisked up to your room, where cabriole legs define the furnishings, and pink marble lines the bathroom.

Unwind on the 2-acre rooftop pool deck, which lies in the shadow of the Eiffel Tower. Or wander the cobblestone streets of Le Boulevard and pick up some bonbons at Lenôtre, or some bling-bling at Cartier.

Paris

Where to eat...

▶ *RECOMMENDED*

Eiffel Tower	XXX	47
Mon Ami Gabi	XX	68

▶ *ALSO*

Le Provençal
Les Artistes Steakhouse
Le Village Buffet

The Strip

PARIS LAS VEGAS
CASINO LEVEL

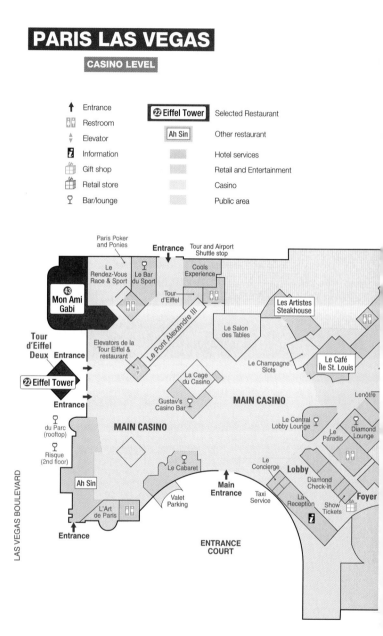

↑	Entrance
Restroom	Restroom
↕	Elevator
?	Information
Gift shop	Gift shop
Retail store	Retail store
♀	Bar/lounge
22 Eiffel Tower	Selected Restaurant
Ah Sin	Other restaurant
	Hotel services
	Retail and Entertainment
	Casino
	Public area

Paris Poker and Ponies

Entrance
Tour and Airport Shuttle stop

Le Rendez-Vous Race & Sport

Le Bar du Sport

Cools Experience

Tour d'Eiffel

43 Mon Ami Gabi

Les Artistes Steakhouse

Tour d'Eiffel Deux Entrance

Le Pont Alexandre III

Le Salon des Tables

Elevators de la Tour Eiffel & restaurant

Le Champagne Slots

Le Café Île St. Louis

22 Eiffel Tower

La Cage du Casino

MAIN CASINO

Lenôtre

Entrance

Gustav's Casino Bar

Le Central Lobby Lounge

Diamond Lounge

du Parc (rooftop)

Le Paradis

Risque (2nd floor)

MAIN CASINO

Le Concierge

Le Cabaret

Lobby

Ah Sin

Main Entrance

Diamond Check-in

Foyer

L'Art de Paris

Valet Parking

Taxi Service

Là Reception

Show Tickets

Entrance

ENTRANCE COURT

LAS VEGAS BOULEVARD

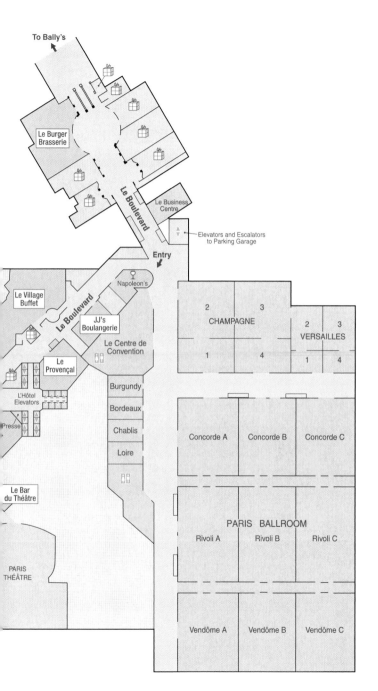

To Bally's

Le Burger Brasserie

Le Boulevard

Le Business Centre

Elevators and Escalators to Parking Garage

Entry

Le Village Buffet

Le Boulevard

Napoleon's

JJ's Boulangerie

Le Centre de Convention

Le Provençal

L'Hôtel Elevators

Burgundy

Bordeaux

Chablis

Loire

Presse

Le Bar du Théâtre

PARIS THÉÂTRE

CHAMPAGNE

2   3

1   4

VERSAILLES

2   3

1   4

Concorde A   Concorde B   Concorde C

PARIS   BALLROOM

Rivoli A   Rivoli B   Rivoli C

Vendôme A   Vendôme B   Vendôme C

193

Planet Hollywood

007

3667 Las Vegas Blvd. S. (at Harmon Ave.)

Phone:	702-785-5555 or 877-333-9474
Fax:	702-785-5511
Web:	www.planethollywoodresort.com
Prices:	**$$$**

2344
Rooms

223
Suites

Aladdin's onion domes and Moorish arches are things of the past, since the bankrupt property sold out to Planet Hollywood. Now the casino displays a high-tech look under a shifting kaleidoscope of colored lights and video screens. It's a cacophony of sights and sounds, the in-your-face design calculated to lure a hip twenty- and thirty-something clientele.

Newly transformed from an Arabian-Sheik to a futuristic-chic décor, this hotel couches more than 2,500 movie-themed rooms and suites inside two 38-story towers. Sizable rooms come equipped with all the modern amenities, including a 27-inch high-definition TV and high-speed Internet connection.

Adjoining the hotel, the Desert Passage mall is undergoing a modern makeover as the Miracle Mile Shops. Expect retailers like H&M and Urban Outfitters to share space with international cuisine options ranging from Polynesian to Greek.

The Strip

Planet Hollywood

Where to eat...

▶ *Recommended*

P.F. Chang's	✕✕	76
Pampas	✕✕	77

▶ *Also*

Spice Market Buffet

The Strip

Treasure Island

008

3300 Las Vegas Blvd. S. (at Spring Mountain Rd.)

Phone: 702-894-7111 or 800-288-7206
Fax: 702-894-7414
Web: www.treasureisland.com
Prices: $$

2665
Rooms

220
Suites

When Steve Wynn debuted this hotel in 1993, the drawbridge from The Strip led to a fanciful world of gold doubloons, one-legged pirates and island hideouts inspired by Robert Louis Stevenson's 1883 novel, *Treasure Island.* Though the replica Mediterranean fishing village still announces the property, you'll no longer find the vestiges of Long John Silver here.

In 2004, the hotel re-branded itself as TI® and replaced the famed pirate's battle with a steamy song-and-dance show, called Sirens of TI®. Rooms and suites were redecorated in pleasing neutrals, with flat-screen TVs and spacious marble baths. Accommodations here go beyond the standard with the signature Elite SensaTIonal© bed, which provides a comfy night's sleep on its pillowtop mattress. If you're a light sleeper, ask for a room on an upper floor—preferably on a side of the building that doesn't face The Strip.

The Strip

MGM Mirage

Where to eat...

▶ *RECOMMENDED*

▶ *ALSO*

The Strip

TREASURE ISLAND

CASINO LEVEL

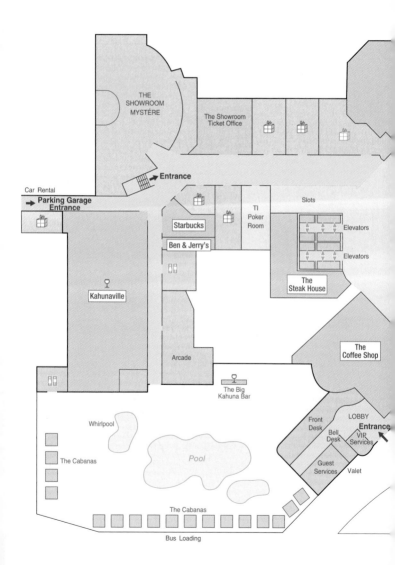

THE SHOWROOM MYSTÉRE

The Showroom Ticket Office

Entrance

Car Rental

Parking Garage Entrance

Slots

Starbucks

TI Poker Room

Ben & Jerry's

Elevators

Elevators

Kahunaville

The Steak House

The Coffee Shop

Arcade

The Big Kahuna Bar

Whirlpool

Front Desk

LOBBY

Entrance

Bell Desk

VIP Services

The Cabanas

Pool

Guest Services

Valet

The Cabanas

Bus Loading

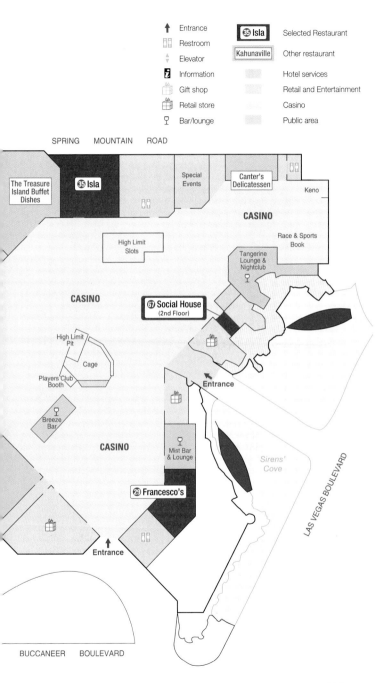

↑	Entrance
🚻	Restroom
↕	Elevator
ℹ️	Information
🎁	Gift shop
🎁	Retail store
🍸	Bar/lounge

35 Isla	Selected Restaurant
Kahunaville	Other restaurant
	Hotel services
	Retail and Entertainment
	Casino
	Public area

SPRING MOUNTAIN ROAD

The Treasure Island Buffet Dishes

35 Isla

Special Events

Canter's Delicatessen

Keno

CASINO

High Limit Slots

Race & Sports Book

Tangerine Lounge & Nightclub 🍸

CASINO

67 Social House (2nd Floor)

High Limit Pit

Cage

Players Club Booth

🍸 Breeze Bar

CASINO

🍸 Mist Bar & Lounge

Sirens' Cove

29 Francesco's

Entrance ↖

Entrance ↑

LAS VEGAS BOULEVARD

BUCCANEER BOULEVARD

Venetian

009

3355 Las Vegas Blvd. S. (bet. Flamingo Rd. & Sands Ave.)

Phone: 702-414-1000 or 877-883-6423
Fax: 702-414-4806
Web: www.venetian.com
Prices: **$$$**

4027
Suites

Erected on the site of the 1952 Sands Hotel, which became the famed home of the Rat Pack, The Venetian had some big shoes to fill—and fill them it has. The sprawling resort, which recasts the Doge's Palace, the Campanile and other Venice landmarks, was launched in May 1999 for $1.5 billion.

La dolce vita envelops guests here, from the inlaid marble floors and the richly detailed frescoes on the lobby ceilings to the gondolas that float passengers through the shopping arcade on a re-creation of the Grand Canal.

More than 4,000 suites fill the property, with a staggering new tower in the works. Decked out in gold, burgundy and royal blue, "standard" suites welcome you into a marble foyer that leads into an elegant bedroom. The sunken living room with its seating area, desk, printer/ fax machine and high-speed Internet access doubles as a work space—ideal for small business meetings.

The Strip

The Venetian

Where to eat...

▶ *Recommended*

Aquaknox	✗✗✗	28
B & B Ristorante	✗✗	30
Bouchon	✗✗	34
David Burke	✗✗	45
Grand Lux Cafe	✗✗	55
Orchid	✗✗✗	74
Pinot Brasserie	✗✗	80
Postrio	✗✗✗	81
Tao	✗✗	99
Taqueria Cañonita	✗✗	100
Valentino	✗✗✗	104

▶ *Also*

Canaletto
Canyon Ranch Café
Delmonico Steakhouse
Enoteca San Marco
Zeffirino

The Strip

THE VENETIAN

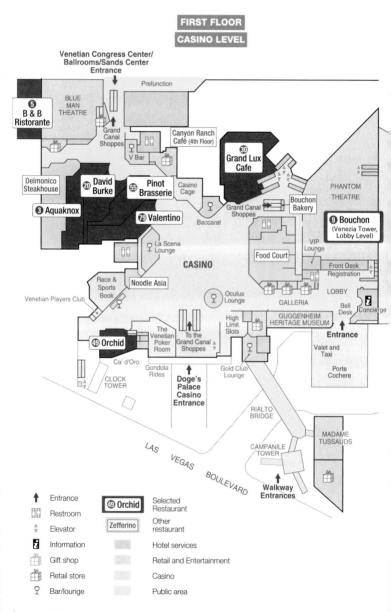

Venetian Congress Center/
Ballrooms/Sands Center
Entrance

Prefunction

BLUE MAN THEATRE

❺ B & B Ristorante

Grand Canal Shoppes

V Bar

Canyon Ranch Café (4th Floor)

❸⓪ Grand Lux Cafe

Delmonico Steakhouse

⓴ David Burke

㊱ Pinot Brasserie

Casino Cage

Bouchon Bakery

PHANTOM THEATRE

❸ Aquaknox

㊲ Valentino

Grand Canal Shoppes

Baccarat

VIP Lounge

❾ Bouchon (Venezia Tower, Lobby Level)

La Scena Lounge

Food Court

CASINO

Front Desk Registration

LOBBY

Venetian Players Club

Race & Sports Book

Noodle Asia

Oculus Lounge

GALLERIA

Bell Desk

ℹ Concierge

㊾ Orchid

The Venetian Poker Room

To the Grand Canal Shoppes

High Limit Slots

GUGGENHEIM HERITAGE MUSEUM

Entrance

Ca' d'Oro

Gondola Rides

Doge's Palace Casino Entrance

Gold Club Lounge

Valet and Taxi

Porte Cochere

CLOCK TOWER

RIALTO BRIDGE

MADAME TUSSAUDS

LAS VEGAS BOULEVARD

CAMPANILE TOWER

Walkway Entrances

↑ Entrance	㊾ Orchid	Selected Restaurant
🚻 Restroom	Zefferino	Other restaurant
↕ Elevator		Hotel services
ℹ Information		Retail and Entertainment
🎁 Gift shop		Casino
🏬 Retail store		Public area
♀ Bar/lounge		

SECOND FLOOR
THE GRAND CANAL SHOPPES

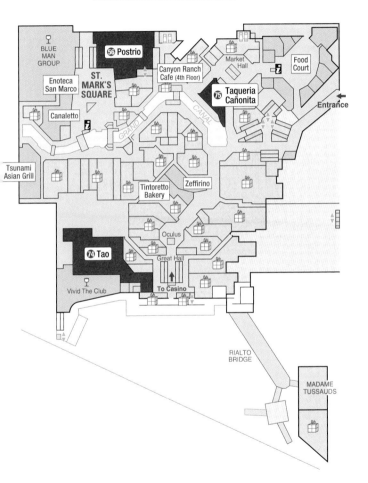

BLUE MAN GROUP

56 Postrio

Enoteca San Marco

ST. MARK'S SQUARE

Canyon Ranch Cafe (4th Floor)

Market Hall

Food Court

Canaletto

75 Taqueria Cañonita

Entrance

Tsunami Asian Grill

GRAND CANAL

Tintoretto Bakery

Zeffirino

Oculus

74 Tao

Great Hall

Vivid The Club

To Casino

RIALTO BRIDGE

MADAME TUSSAUDS

203

Wynn

010

3131 Las Vegas Blvd. S. (at Sands Ave.)

Phone: 702-770-7100 or 888-320-9966
Fax: 702-770-1571
Web: www.wynnlasvegas.com
Prices: $$$$

2359
Rooms

357
Suites

What kind of a hotel can you build for $2.7 billion? To see the answer, look up the north end of The Strip to the curving bronze-glass monolith named for its creator, Steve Wynn. "The man who made Las Vegas" opened this resort on the site of the old Desert Inn in April 2005. With a Tom Fazio-designed golf course, designer boutiques, and a Ferrari-Maserati dealership on-site, Wynn's posh playground leaves little to be desired.

At 640 square feet, a Resort Room here tops the "most-spacious" list. Egyptian cotton linens, a robe and slippers, a down duvet, and a pillowtop bed provide sumptuous comfort; a fax machine, three phone lines, and a flat-screen TV with Internet capability and wireless keyboard cater to business travelers.

Be sure to catch a showing of the water-based spectacle Le Rêve. The show takes its name from a Picasso painting (part of Steve Wynn's art collection), which is displayed in the hotel.

The Strip

Wynn Resorts

Where to eat...

The Strip

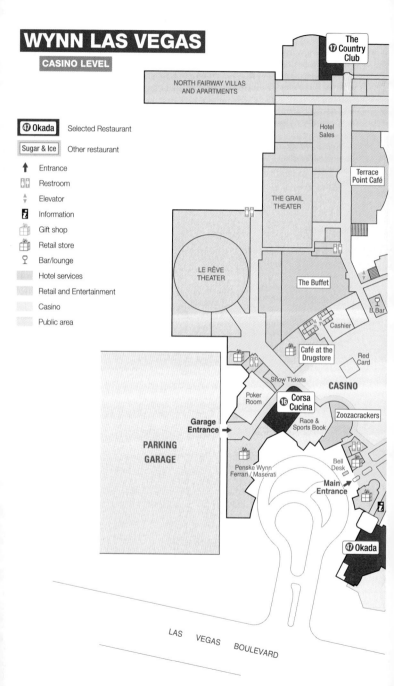

WYNN LAS VEGAS
CASINO LEVEL

⑰ Okada — Selected Restaurant

Sugar & Ice — Other restaurant

- ↑ Entrance
- 🚻 Restroom
- ⇕ Elevator
- ℹ Information
- 🎁 Gift shop
- 🏬 Retail store
- 🍸 Bar/lounge
- Hotel services
- Retail and Entertainment
- Casino
- Public area

The ⑰ Country Club

NORTH FAIRWAY VILLAS AND APARTMENTS

Hotel Sales

Terrace Point Café

THE GRAIL THEATER

LE RÊVE THEATER

The Buffet

B.Bar

Cashier

Café at the Drugstore

Red Card

Show Tickets

CASINO

Poker Room

⑯ Corsa Cucina

Zoozacrackers

Race & Sports Book

Garage Entrance →

PARKING GARAGE

Penske Wynn Ferrari / Maserati

Bell Desk

Main → Entrance

⑰ Okada

LAS VEGAS BOULEVARD

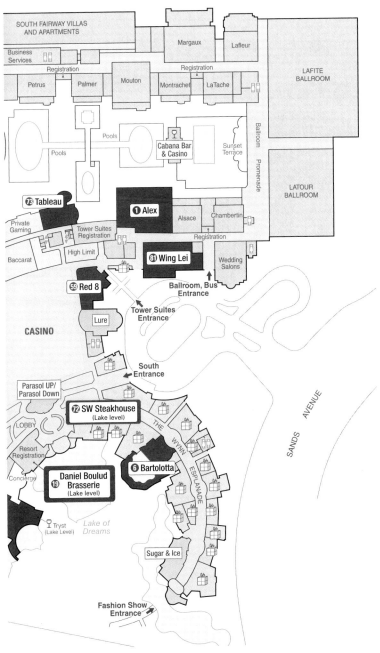

SOUTH FAIRWAY VILLAS
AND APARTMENTS

Business
Services

Margaux

Lafleur

Registration

Petrus

Palmer

Mouton

Registration

Montrachet

LaTache

LAFITE
BALLROOM

Pools

Pools

Pools

Cabana Bar
& Casino

Sunset
Terrace

Ballroom Promenade

LATOUR
BALLROOM

73 Tableau

Private
Gaming

Tower Suites
Registration

1 Alex

Alsace

Chambertin

Baccarat

High Limit

81 Wing Lei

Registration

Wedding
Salons

59 Red 8

Ballroom, Bus
Entrance

Tower Suites
Entrance

Lure

CASINO

South
Entrance

Parasol UP/
Parasol Down

72 SW Steakhouse
(Lake level)

THE

WYNN

ESPLANADE

SANDS AVENUE

LOBBY

Resort
Registration

6 Bartolotta

Concierge

19 Daniel Boulud
Brasserie
(Lake level)

Tryst
(Lake Level)

Lake of
Dreams

Sugar & Ice

Fashion Show
Entrance

Bally's

3645 Las Vegas Blvd. S. (at E. Flamingo Rd.)

Phone: 702-967-4111 or 800-634-3434
Fax: N/A
Web: www.ballyslasvegas.com
Prices: $$

2549
Rooms

265
Suites

Bally's

Cary Grant, Fred MacMurray and Raquel Welch hosted this property's ribbon-cutting ceremony in 1973, when it opened as the MGM Grand. Bally's Manufacturing Corporation purchased the hotel and renamed it in 1981.

Located in the middle of The Strip, Bally's incorporates two 26-story towers filled with more than 2,800 rooms and suites. Standard guestrooms measure 450 square feet, and all the expected amenities apply (there are no mini bars in the standard rooms, but the hotel will rent you a small refrigerator for $10 a day). A recent multimillion-dollar facelift has spiffed up the accommodations with tasteful overstuffed furniture, light woods and marble baths.

For classic entertainment, Donn Arden's Jubilee! hearkens back to the classic Vegas revue, replete with leggy lovelies scantily clad in bejeweled costumes and elaborate headpieces (how *do* they keep those things on?).

The Strip

Flamingo

012

3555 Las Vegas Blvd. S. (at E. Flamingo Rd.)

Phone:	888-902-9929 or 800-732-2111
Fax:	702-733-3528
Web:	www.flamingolasvegas.com
Prices:	$$

3466
Rooms

176
Suites

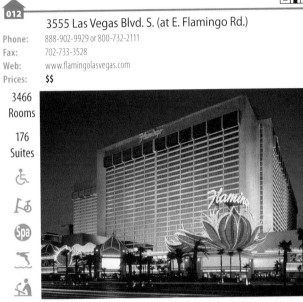

Flamingo

In 1946, when mobster Benjamin "Bugsy" Siegel debuted his $6-million "real class joint," it was touted as the world's most luxurious hotel. Despite its location in the middle of the desert, the Flamingo lured players with its sterling-silver place settings and tuxedo-clad—even down to the janitors—staff.

The 105-room "House that Bugsy Built" has since been transformed into a multitower resort (the trapdoors and tunnels that Siegel built into his personal suite disappeared in the course of the expansions). Blazing pink neon still illuminates the hotel at night, though earth tones replace the pink hues once found inside.

Comfortable rooms are on the small side, their floor-to-ceiling windows overlooking The Strip. Tech-savvy guests may reserve a "Go Deluxe" room, equipped with an iPod docking station, a DVD/CD player, a 42-inch flat-screen TV, and wireless Internet access.

The Strip

Luxor

3900 Las Vegas Blvd. S. (at Reno Ave.)

Phone:	702-262-4444 or 888-777-0188
Fax:	702-262-4404
Web:	www.luxor.com
Prices:	$$

4111
Rooms

430
Suites

MGM Mirage

Walk like an Egyptian into this massive, 30-story pyramid, beneath a 110-foot-tall replica of the Sphinx. A scale model of the Great Pyramid of Giza, Luxor abounds inside with temple façades, hieroglyphic panels and murals depicting life in ancient Egypt. It's quite an impressive scene, gazing up at the interior of the structure from the Atrium level above the casino, where theaters, restaurants, and King Tut's Tomb and Museum are located.

To reach their rooms, guests board "inclinators," elevators that travel up the interior slope of the 350-foot pyramid at a 39-degree angle. Egyptian-inspired décor runs to red and gold hues, inlaid wood furnishings and pale marble. Many of the tower rooms are newly renovated.

Mandalay Place shopping mall fills a skybridge that connects Luxor to Mandalay Bay, while Nurture, the Spa at Luxor, pampers guests with treatments fit for a Pharoah.

Monte Carlo

3770 Las Vegas Blvd. S. (bet. Harmon & Tropicana Aves.)

Phone:	702-730-7777 or 888-529-4828
Fax:	702-730-7350
Web:	www.montecarlo.com
Prices:	$$

2743 Rooms

259 Suites

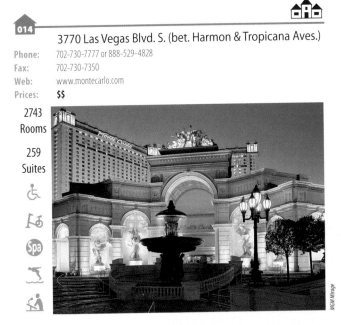

MGM Mirage

Set back from the boulevard, the Monte Carlo evokes an understated elegance compared to more flamboyant Strip properties. The refined image will hit home when you enter the marble-lined lobby, hung with crystal chandeliers and adorned with potted palms. It will be reinforced if you dine at Andre's *(see restaurant listing)*, which is decked out like a French château. Think of James Bond in *Casino Royale* (filmed in Monaco) and you've got the picture.

This hotel boasts just over 3,000 guest rooms, newly renovated with contemporary fittings, complete with flat-screen TVs and high-speed Internet access. Suites add amenities such as dining rooms, wet bars, remote-control lighting, and marble bathrooms with whirlpool tubs and steam showers. For guests who stay on the top floor, accommodations—including two penthouse suites—come with personalized concierge service as well as privacy gained from key-card access.

The Strip

Stratosphere

2000 Las Vegas Blvd. S. (bet. Sahara & St. Louis Aves.)

Phone:	702-380-7777 or 800-998-6937
Fax:	702-380-7732
Web:	www.stratospherehotel.com
Prices:	$

2313
Rooms

131
Suites

Stratosphere Las Vegas

Stratosphere marks the north end of The Strip with its landmark 1,149-foot-tall tower, touted as the tallest building west of the Mississippi River. It's all about height here: the observation deck offers a dizzying panorama of The Strip and the surrounding valley; Top of the World restaurant *(see restaurant listing)* serves dinner with a killer view; the Chapel in the Clouds accommodates lofty weddings; and, for thrill seekers, sky-high rides Big Shot, X-Scream and Insanity all pack one heck of an adrenaline punch.

As for the rest of this 1996 property, it's not so thrilling, but it does offer comfortable, clean and quiet rooms for a comparative song (under $100 a night)—especially given its location. No matter that your room isn't lined with marble and fancy fabrics; with all the money you'll save, you can afford a gourmet dinner out, or another night at the blackjack table.

The Strip

Carriage House

105 E. Harmon Ave. (bet. Audrie St. & Las Vegas Blvd. S.)

Phone: 702-798-1020 or 800-221-2301 ext. 65
Fax: 702-798-1020 ext. 112
Web: www.carriagehouselasvegas.com
Prices: $

154 Rooms

&

©Mark Gibson

This non-gaming property offers an inexpensive alternative to the high-end properties along Las Vegas Boulevard, located one block to the west.

Carriage House may lack many of the amenities found in the larger resorts—there's no room service, no conference center, no lush landscaped grounds—but standard (or "deluxe" in the hotel's parlance) rooms here are thoughtfully outfitted with a fully equipped kitchenette, a DVD and VCR, a hair dryer, a safe, an iron and ironing board, and complimentary high-speed Internet access. One-bedroom suites accommodate families with a queen-size sofa bed in the living area. For outdoor recreation, head for the heated pool and whirlpool, or the lighted tennis/basketball court.

If you don't mind doing without a few luxuries, the Carriage House is a place where you can save a few dollars to splurge on dinner or a show elsewhere in town.

East of The Strip

Green Valley Ranch

2300 Paseo Verde Dr. (at I-215), Henderson

Phone: 702-617-7777 or 866-782-9487
Fax: 702-617-7748
Web: www.greenvalleyranchresort.com
Prices: $$

490
Rooms

Station Casinos

You won't miss out on the action at Green Valley Ranch. Located 7 miles east of The Strip via I-215, this Mediterranean-style resort has it all: a casino, a 10,000-square-foot European day spa, a cinema complex, even a working vineyard.

Nearly 500 spacious rooms, made plush by down comforters, luxurious linens and feather beds, are divided between the East and West towers. Dark wood furnishings uphold the ritzy feel, while large windows look out over the surrounding mountains.

In front of the hotel stretches a "Main Street" of shops and restaurants; the "backyard" holds an 8-acre pool complex with a sand beach. Restaurant options cater to carnivores, between Hank's Fine Steak & Martinis and nearby Lucille's Smokehouse Barbeque *(see restaurant listing for both)*. For entertainment, you can dance the night away at the hip Whiskey Bar.

The resort provides shuttle service to and from McCarran International Airport and The Strip.

East of The Strip

Hard Rock

018

4455 Paradise Rd. (at Harmon Ave.)

Phone:	702-693-5000 or 800-473-7625
Fax:	702-693-5588
Web:	www.hardrockhotel.com
Prices:	$$

583
Rooms

63
Suites

This place really rocks. From the rock 'n roll music that blares 24/7 to the raised central bar in the casino, the Hard Rock is no staid retreat. It packs in the twenty-somethings, who appreciate that Kurt Cobain's grungy garb passes for décor, and mind-blowing 25-foot-tall speaker bays amplify the sounds of the live bands that perform at The Joint.

You'll see some heavenly bodies at the Beach Club, lounging in private cabanas or trying their luck at swim-up blackjack. "Rehab Sunday" at the pool is a raucous adults-only bash. Even the rooms rock, with a Bose CD stereo system and a plasma TV featuring music channels. On-site restaurants range from prime sirloin at A.J.'s Steakhouse to fusion fare at Simon's Kitchen & Bar. There's also premium sushi at Nobu and modern Mexican at Pink Taco (see restaurant listing for all four).

The hotel's new owners plan to rock on with a new tower, a convention center, and more concert and retail space.

East of The Strip

Hilton

019

3000 Paradise Rd. (bet. Convention Center Dr. & Karen Ave.)

Phone: 702-732-5111 or 888-737-7117
Fax: 702-732-5778
Web: www.lvhilton.com
Prices: **$$**

2833
Rooms

124
Suites

Las Vegas Hilton

Convenient to the Las Vegas Convention Center, the Hilton claims the distinction of having hosted Elvis Presley's Sin City debut in July 1969 (though the hotel was then known as the International). Elvis may have left the building, but his legend lives on in the bronze statue recently reinstalled in the hotel. Today other entertainment legends hold sway here, notably Barry Manilow, who is headlining through 2008 at the 1,700-seat Hilton Theater.

Vegas glitz is in short supply in this off-the-Strip property. Rooms are basic and conservative in decoration, and you won't find the type of service you'd be treated to at a swankier Strip hotel. Even so, the Hilton has some nice amenities—a large outdoor pool, a fitness center and spa, a salon, even a putting green and a video arcade—for the price. Trekkies will love the virtual-reality ride, Star Trek: The Experience.

Loews Lake Las Vegas

101 Montelago Blvd. (off Lake Mead Pkwy.), Henderson

Phone: 702-567-6000 or 800-235-6397
Fax: 702-567-6067
Web: www.loewshotels.com
Prices: $$$

447 Rooms

46 Suites

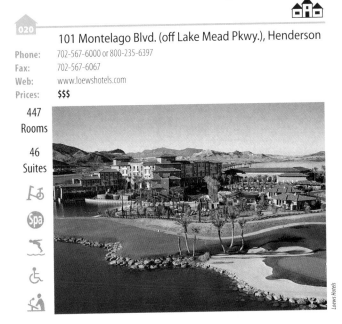

Loews Hotels

Forget about gambling and The Strip. Head east and place your bets on Loews instead. There's no casino here, but once you look out on the lovely waters of Lake Las Vegas with the rugged peaks in the distance, you won't miss all those clanging slot machines.

A Moroccan theme pervades, with plenty of fountains and colorful tiled walls. All rooms come with cotton linens, terry robes, flat-screen TVs, in-room video games, and a safe that will accommodate your laptop. For around-the-clock enjoyment of the natural beauty just outside, splurge on a lake-view room.

Don't leave the kids or the pets at home; both are welcome at Loews. The Kids Club tailors activities to the young set, while the hotel proves its love of animals with a special room-service menu. While your four-legged friends are noshing on Bow Wow tenderloin of beef and Kitty's salmon supreme, you can savor Asian-inspired seafood at Marssa *(see restaurant listing)*.

East of The Strip

Platinum

211 E. Flamingo Rd. (at Koval Ln.)

Phone:	702-365-5000 or 877-211-9211
Fax:	702-365-5000
Web:	www.theplatinumhotel.com
Prices:	$$

255
Suites

Platinum

If gambling's not your cup of tea, you'll find this non-gaming, non-smoking, all-suites hotel to be right up your quiet alley. Premiered in October 2006, the Platinum shines with a full range of services and amenities, including an indoor/outdoor pool, a state-of-the-art fitness center, a noteworthy restaurant *(see restaurant listing)*, and the 4,000-square-foot WELL spa.

The residential atmosphere here is couched in urban-chic style in three tiers of spacious suites. All hit the mother lode with a gourmet kitchen, a Bose sound system, an outdoor terrace, a living room with sofa bed, a whirlpool tub, and high-speed Internet access (both wired and wireless). A washer and dryer and a fireplace enhance the larger suites (which run from 1,083 to 2,165 square feet).

When you're itching for more action, you'll find the glitz and gambling of The Strip less than two blocks away.

East of The Strip

Ritz-Carlton Lake Las Vegas

1610 Lake Las Vegas Pkwy. (off Lake Mead Pkwy.), Henderson

Phone: 702-567-4700 or 800-241-3333
Fax: 702-567-4777
Web: www.ritz-carlton.com
Prices: $$$

314 Rooms

35 Suites

The Ritz-Carlton

Location, location, location: these are the three best reasons to stay at the Ritz-Carlton Lake Las Vegas. A mere 17-mile drive east of The Strip brings you to this serene oasis, arranged on the shore of a 320-acre privately owned lake. The resort's architecture recalls the towns of Tuscany—and even spans the water with its own re-creation of Florence's Ponte Vecchio.

Smooth, personalized service is the signature of the Ritz. Guests are addressed by name, and every effort is made to insure a memorable stay. "Standard" rooms belie the name, feathering these nests with warm pastels, Frette linens, and marble and granite in the baths. For extra pampering, book one of the 65 Club Level rooms.

Medici Café *(see restaurant listing)* complements the Tuscan theme with its garden terrace and contemporary cuisine. Golf and water sports suffice for active guests, while the spa, the pool, and the white-sand beach offer ample opportunities to relax.

East of The Strip

Westin Casuarina

160 E. Flamingo Rd. (at Koval Ln.)

Phone:	702-836-5900
Fax:	702-836-9776
Web:	www.starwoodhotels.com
Prices:	$$

816
Rooms

10
Suites

Starwood Hotels

With a modest 826 rooms, the Westin Casuarina is in a class apart from the megaresorts on The Strip. The hotel accommodates business travelers with 25,000 square feet of meeting space, and its proximity to the Las Vegas Convention Center (only a mile away). A 24-hour fitness center is conveniently located near the meeting rooms.

Of course, there's a casino (with 10 table games and slot machines galore), all-day dining (either at the casual restaurant or in your room) and free self-parking. You can swim laps in the heated pool, work out on-site, or balance your chi with a Reiki treatment at the Hibiscus Spa.

In the pet-friendly rooms you'll find warm woods, sleek lines and soothing palettes. Dual showerheads, coffeemakers, in-room safes, fluffy towels and robes, and Westin's Heavenly Bed® with its 10-layer pillowtop mattress round out the creature comforts.

East of The Strip

JW Marriott Resort

221 N. Rampart Blvd. (off Summerlin Pkwy.)

Phone:	702-869-7777 or 877-869-8777
Fax:	702-869-7339
Web:	www.jwlasvegasresort.com
Prices:	$$

469 Rooms

79 Suites

JW Marriott

The suburb of Summerlin is home to this sprawling resort, which boasts stunning views of Red Rock Canyon. On 54 acres, the complex is connected by interior walkways through the casino or via outdoor paths that traverse the lushly landscaped grounds.

Targeting tranquility rather than late-night partying, the Marriott seems worlds away from The Strip. The Mediterranean-style venue attracts groups for business meetings, as well as a gaggle of golfers who come to play the nine courses nearby.

A marble foyer introduces guests to roomy chambers tastefully appointed in quiet shades of beige. Feather beds, walk-in closets, whirlpool tubs and separate rain showers are a few of the frills.

Whether fitness, beauty or wellness is your focus, you can address your needs at the Aquae Sulis Spa. Cuisine options range from pub fare at J.C. Woologhan to sushi at Shizen *(see restaurant listing for both)*.

West of The Strip

Orleans

4500 W. Tropicana Ave. (at Arville St.)

Phone:	702-365-7111 or 800-675-3267
Fax:	702-365-7500
Web:	www.orleanscasino.com
Prices:	$

1867
Rooms

19
Suites

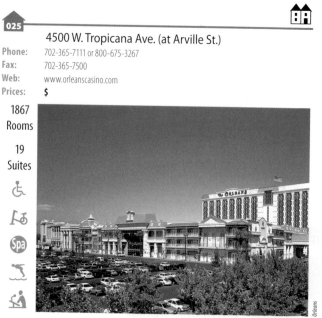

Orleans

With its lively French Quarter theme, the Orleans provides comfortable, quiet and well-maintained rooms—"petite suites" as the hotel bills them—that don't skimp on size with 450 square feet as the standard. Complimentary valet parking and free shuttle service to The Strip are two of the more attractive amenities.

You won't want for things to do here. The Orleans is known for its 70-lane bowling center, complete with a pro shop in case you forgot to bring your bowling shirt. Then there's the 9,000-seat Orleans Arena next door, which hosts everything from monster-truck rallies to championship boxing matches to the circus. In the hotel's showroom, you can catch music acts (the Beach Boys, Neil Sedaka, The Temptations) and comedians (George Carlin, the Smothers Brothers). And if you just want to kick back, head for the spa or the pool ... and let the good times roll.

West of The Strip

Palms

4321 W. Flamingo Rd. (at Wynn Rd.)

Phone: 702-942-7777 or 866-942-7777
Fax: 702-942-7001
Web: www.palms.com
Prices: **$$**

573
Rooms

147
Suites

Palms Casino Resort

The young and the hip party at the Palms, where the exclusive Playboy Club sets the tone with high-stakes gaming and "bunny" dealers. Between Rain's raised dance floor, Ghostbar's indoor/outdoor lounge and skydeck, and Moon—the newest venue—with its retractable penthouse roof, you can indulge in some serious club-hopping without leaving the property.

Guests may spend limited time in their rooms, but when they do, they can count on luminous contemporary quarters filled with upscale amenities. Part of a recent makeover, the Fantasy Tower fosters a don't-ask-don't-tell attitude with its Party Floor suites, and Sky Villas equipped with media and exercise rooms, pantries and full bars. Expect "service on the spot" at the touch of a button on your room phone.

Gourmets can choose among restaurants that roam to Europe at Alizé and Nove Italiano, then back to North America with Garduños for Mexican fare and N9NE for hearty steaks *(see restaurant listing for all four)*.

West of The Strip

Red Rock Resort

11011 W. Charleston Blvd. (at I-215)

Phone:	702-797-7777 or 866-767-7773
Fax:	702-797-7831
Web:	www.redrocklasvegas.com
Prices:	**$$$**

814
Rooms

45
Suites

Station Casinos

One of the city's newest resorts, this sophisticated retreat flaunts its enviable setting near Red Rock Canyon National Conservation Area. The spa uses the park as a playground, offering a full menu of kayak and bike tours, hiking and horseback riding, and rock climbing and river rafting. Among the on-site dining choices, Terra Rossa *(see restaurant listing)* plays on the property's name while featuring tasty Italian fare.

The dramatic lobby drips with inlaid marble and cascading crystal chandeliers, while zebra-striped wood paneling and modern art adorn the hallways. Rooms are spacious and boldly contemporary, rife with rich tones and textures, and floor-to-ceiling windows that frame red-rock panoramas. Take a soak in the tub while watching the flat-screen TV mounted above, then slide into your robe and slippers.

In the 3-acre "backyard" you can lounge by the pool, where attendants will supply towels, refreshments and even reading material.

West of The Strip

Rio

028

3700 W. Flamingo Rd. (at Valley View Blvd.)

Phone: 702-777-7777 or 866-746-7671
Fax: 702-777-6462
Web: www.riolasvegas.com
Prices: $$

2563
Suites

Rio

Every day is *Carnivale* at the Rio. From the vibrant Brazilian décor to the 100,000 square feet of gaming space, there's no shortage of action off The Strip here. The Rio's spirit is embodied by the Masquerade Show in the Sky. This raucous music-and-dance show, performed on floats suspended from the ceiling above the casino floor, is perhaps the best free entertainment in town.

Every room is a suite at the Rio. Starting at 600 square feet and stretching up to 1,600 square feet, accommodations are decked out with custom-designed furnishings and antiques. Upgraded suites have wet bars, while all have a refrigerator and a balcony.

A one-stop entertainment destination, the Rio hosts the interactive production Tony n' Tina's Wedding and the macabre comedy of Penn and Teller—not to mention the Chippendales' hunky all-male revue. Rio's restaurants include Antonio's for lovers of Italian food and Gaylord India for more exotic tastes (*see restaurant listing for both*).

West of The Strip

225

Golden Nugget

129 Fremont St. (at 1st St.)

Phone:	702-385-7111 or 800-846-5336
Fax:	702-386-8362
Web:	www.goldennugget.com
Prices:	$

1874
Rooms

33
Suites

Golden Nugget

Opened in 1946, the Golden Nugget is a Downtown dowager. Despite her age, this lady manages to exude the spirit of old Las Vegas without appearing outdated. Thank the $100-million facelift, which is gussying up the grand dame from head to toe.

Rooms in the two towers are now dressed in pale florals and outfitted with high-speed Internet. Downstairs, the pool has been transformed into a tropical oasis, complete with The Tank, where you can swim nose to snout with beady-eyed sharks, separated only by a few inches of reinforced glass. Another addition is the Grotto trattoria, which joins Vic & Anthony's steakhouse *(see restaurant listing for both)* as part of the hotel's dining lineup.

And what would the Golden Nugget be without its icon, the nearly 62-pound mass of gold known as the "Hand of Faith"? This artifact resides in a quiet corner off the lobby, where it provides the backdrop for a favorite photo op.

Downtown

Main Street Station

200 N. Main St. (at Stewart Ave.)

Phone: 702-387-1896 or 800-465-0711
Fax: 702-386-4466
Web: www.mainstreetcasino.com
Prices: $

406
Rooms

14
Suites

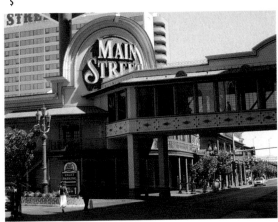

©Mark Gibson

Victorian-era civility lives on at Main Street Station. Located just a few blocks from the computer-generated sound-and-light show known as the Fremont Street Experience, this casino cashes in on the ambience of a bygone era.

In the common areas, dark mahogany wood, stained-glass skylights, period antiques and vintage Pullman cars recall the turn-of-the-20th-century railroad heyday. Renovated rooms, by contrast, are contemporary in style, with dark wood armoires, cushioned armchairs, and white plantation shutters on the windows. The hotel doesn't offer room service, Internet access or mini bars in the guestrooms, but there are three dining options downstairs (the Triple 7 Restaurant and Brewery serves breakfast from midnight until 7am), and you can guard your valuables inside the in-room safe.

Trains whistling by on the active tracks nearby only add to the railroad theme.

Downtown

Notes

Notes

Notes

Notes

Notes

Notes

Notes

Notes

Notes

Notes

Notes

Notes

Notes

Notes

Notes

Notes